Guidance Memo

Daisaku Ikeda

Translated by
George M. Williams

World Tribune Press

©1975
Copyright by The World Tribune Press
Santa Monica, California
Library of Congress catalogue card no. 75-13664
ISBN 0-915678-00-4
Lithographed in the United States of America

Table of Contents

PREFACE 5
FOREWORD 6
LEADERS 9
ICHINEN 69
UNITY 111
PRACTICE 159
HOPE 197
WOMANHOOD 227
CULTURE 251
GLOSSARY 276
INDEX 280

Preface

There have been repeated requests that the *Guidance Memo* column in the Seikyo Press be reprinted in book form.

Frankly, I was surprised that the Seikyo Press reporters wanted to publish my casual remarks in the newspaper. However, I had no objection, if it would be of any help at all to my fellow members.

Still, I found that in print, some of the guidance seemed out of context, and I was afraid that readers might be confused. In order to be as clear as possible, I asked for the opportunity to make revisions before the book was published.

Being an ordinary man, I have no spectacular or outstanding guidance to offer. Yet, I am continually praying that my fellow members will take the right course in faith and in life, based on the supreme teachings of Nichiren Daishonin. If this book encourages one person even a little in his practice or furthers Kosen-rufu by one step, I shall be very happy.

Daisaku Ikeda
President of the Sokagakkai

Foreword

In his travels throughout the world, President Ikeda has met with millions of people and taken the time to give them lasting hope and courage. Because of his understanding of human struggles gained as a youth during WW II, he has become a great pacifist. He has traveled the world over many times, visiting over forty nations to restore true humanism to a world that has grown cold and mechanical. His vision of a peaceful and prosperous world is the foundation of his belief and the driving force of his great efforts on behalf of people everywhere.

His warmth and compassion win the hearts of people from all walks of life, whether they are statesmen or everyday laborers. He is loved as the leader of millions of people whom he has encouraged. The transcripts of his conversations over the years have been compiled in this *Guidance Memo.* I sincerely hope that this new English translation will become the mainstay of faith for all who read it.

One of the sutras reads, "Infinite meanings come from one Law." In the same way, the true value of President Ikeda's guidance is its relevance to people of all ages, nationalities and cultural heritages. Buddhism began with one man's search for an end to suffering and unhappiness in life. Today, President Ikeda is the foremost spokesman of the wisdom contained in Buddhist teachings. In the pages of this book, the reader can find clues to happiness and fulfillment in life, which can be summarized in one phrase — "to create value." That is the essence of Buddhism, and the wisdom contained in this volume.

There are many "How to" books that are popular these days, but none of them can tell a person how to change his destiny and become happy. For that, you have to look to Nichiren Daishonin's life-philosophy. This *Guidance Memo*, reflecting the great life-philosophy of true Buddhism, offers answers to the many problems of life.

The guidance in this book was given to individuals with different problems, circumstances, questions and different levels of faith. The reader can understand and apply this guidance to his own life only through a sound practice and sincere faith in this philosophy. Think of it this way — if you merely memorize recipes from a cookbook, you will not become a great chef; if you practice them in a kitchen, you can master them. Using faith to understand this guidance, you can use it in your daily practice. With such a foundation, I sincerely hope you will become victorious, not only in your campaigns in NSA, but also in everything you undertake in your daily life.

George M. Williams
General Director

Chapter One: Leaders

A new type of leader

Those leaders who developed through their practice to the Gohonzon are of a new type. The dominant figures in Communist revolutions rose through their belief in a materialistic ideology. However, theirs is a philosophy of the past.

Capitalism and the Christian tradition have formed the background for leaders in most free nations. Yet these leaders hold nothing fresh for the people.

As of now, there are no world leaders trained in the strict world of Buddhism, who embrace the Gohonzon and uphold the life-philosophy of *Shiki Shin Funi*. The first-class leaders who appear in the future will be those who practice to the Gohonzon.

Many well-known leaders are pioneers who are greatly influencing our world today. But they are removed from the hearts of the people who support them. A new type of leader is one who embraces the same philosophy, the same faith and the same objective as the people, thereby raising each of them to his own level, according to the principle of consistency from beginning to end *(Honmatsu Kukyo-to)*.

Throughout history, fame-seeking and hero-worship have given rise to the idea that leaders are great and the general public ignorant and powerless. This concept is wrong and contradicts true democracy. Individuals must each awaken and unite voluntarily. Some of them will be statesmen and others, scientists or artists. They will become true leaders of the public, with whom they are working directly. At the same time, the people who support them must become leaders, too. This is the new principle for both leaders and the people.

Essentials for leadership

The first requirement for leaders is absolute faith. Absolute faith means declaring the benefits of the Gohonzon, even in the face of great obstacles, so that the Daishonin's Buddhism will spread, as well as realizing that this is your fundamental mission.

Second is a sense of responsibility. A leader should love his members, protect them and encourage them warmly. He is responsible for their happiness. His sense of responsibility is deepened by his affection, so that whatever obstacles they meet, the leader will feel, "I'll never let my members down." Being irresponsible shows a lack of mercy.

⁓⁓⁓

Thirdly, a leader must be broad-minded. He should be capable of understanding his members' individual situations, putting himself in their place. He should have the determination to hear any problem and guide any type of person to establish firm faith and become happy. The sutra calls this "donning the robe of gentleness and forbearance."

⁓⁓⁓

Fourthly, leaders need to be impartial. They must not be swayed by their feelings or by personal considerations. They should give a fair hearing to reasonable suggestions, but firmly protest mistaken views or emotionalism, even that of their seniors.

Leaders should not cater to people who flatter them. One who cannot spot cheap tricks, lies and sneakiness is not a great leader. A good leader can tell how hard each of his members is working for Kosen-rufu, even if their efforts are inconspicuous. He can put the right person in the right place.

Finally, leaders need self-confidence. Self-confidence includes determination, courage and decisiveness. A leader must have the self-confidence to protect his members, give them hope and enable them to advance cheerfully.

Wisdom and courage

A person of wisdom and courage is a true leader. Today, living and working in society with faith in the supreme Law *(Myoho)* as your basis exemplifies courage and wisdom. A passage from the *Gosho* reads, *Employ no strategy other than that of the Lotus Sutra.* The ultimate wisdom is the wisdom of Buddhahood. Only faith will enable you to tap this wisdom and courage.

The vitality which emerges through faith also includes wisdom. Nichiren Daishonin wrote in the *Gosho, Believers in the Lotus Sutra will know the worldly law.* Faith enables us to employ wisdom effectively in all situations throughout our lives.

Courage is indispensable in the fight for Kosen-rufu. There is no place for cowardice. Great leaders of the supreme Law are people of outstanding wisdom and courage. Gakkai members meet these qualifications, so advance with confidence in your own courage and wisdom.

Building "a castle of capable men" means producing a galaxy of leaders of the supreme Law, leaders who have achieved their human revolution through faith in the Gohonzon. Developing capable individuals is both the starting point and the end result of any endeavor.

Courage without wisdom is mere savagery, and wisdom without the courage to practice will prove abstract and fruitless. Ultimately, you need both wisdom and courage.

Advance with the confidence that so long as you continue to practice, you are already a capable person.

Impartial but considerate

In the organization, leaders must be absolutely impartial. They should be capable of recognizing sound arguments, emotional statements and opinions for what they are.

However, after firmly stating what is right, a good leader should warmly encourage each person. Developing this capacity is part of a leader's training.

When giving guidance, it's fine to show your own strong personality, but you must thoroughly convince the members and reassure them.

Great leaders do not criticize each error on the part of their staff. They praise them for what they have done well. There are other people who will criticize the staff.

Leadership requires humanism. Let your juniors put their ideas into practice freely and openly but at the same time, steer them in the right direction.

Daimoku, mercy and wisdom

Just because someone becomes a leader, it does not mean he has perfect faith. Leadership positions are a means to help people develop. Faith is a matter of lifelong practice. To develop as a leader suited to the coming era, you must study voluntarily and every day, chant more Daimoku than anyone else.

A leader who abides by formality, judges people's value by their position or pretends to have strong faith is cheap and calculating. He does not have real faith. Eventually, he will reach a deadlock and lose his vitality. A leader's first concern is to chant Daimoku sincerely and have an exemplary practice himself.

Secondly, there are members who won't listen or who want to go their own way. Convincing them of the value of guidance is the same thing as Shakubuku. Leaders would be unnecessary if new members could fully develop their faith without receiving guidance. Realizing this, you should lead your members with patience and courage. The *Ichinen* to make them understand faith is equivalent to mercy.

Thirdly, use your wisdom. Don't be stiff and awkward, indecisive or lacking in confidence. Using good judgment according to the circumstances is called *Zuien Shinnyo-no Chi.* Through common sense and your own experience, you can confidently lead people in the direction you judge best. Members will then feel reassured.

A devoted few

In a chapter, the system of a devoted few refers to the district leaders uniting around their chapter chief, forming a nucleus for the growth of the whole chapter.

The system of a devoted few does not merely mean a small number. It is a formula by which capable leaders unite to organize and lead the entire membership, however large. Otherwise they become a mob.

Big business has also adopted the system of a devoted few. Qualified staff in the top echelons of prosperous companies have the task of effectively directing all employees.

The forces of Oda Nobunaga[1] who won the battle of Okehazama relied on the system of a devoted few. Imagawa Yoshimoto's men, though far greater in number, were just a loose, helter-skelter gathering of various armies. If ten or twenty excellent generals had united to form a strong nucleus with Yoshimoto as their central figure, they could have directed those huge forces at will. The Imagawa armies were defeated, in part, because they lacked such unity.

The public mind

A sharp mind alone won't make you a leader. You have to be in touch with the climate of popular opinion and be capable of distinguishing between majority and minority opinions.

Your own ideas are often abstract and fail to match the will of the public. A good leader always knows what the people really want.

---

[1] Oda Nobunaga (1534-82)—tried to unify Japan during the civil war period. Defeated Imagawa Yoshimoto, one of the most powerful warlords, at Okehazama in 1560.

Newspapers reflect various aspects of public interest. People may seek out the latest news or the further details of a past event. Reports on royalty, for example, excite people's interest, though this news is often repetitious. This reveals the public sentiment.

The eyes to see people

A man can develop remarkably, even under adverse circumstances, when he awakens to his mission and a great objective.

When we're close to another person, we tend to notice his faults and even point them out. However, once you start finding fault with someone, there's no end to it. Human beings are imperfect. Instead, we should respect one another, compensate for each other's shortcomings and bring out each other's strong points.

When you evaluate someone, ask yourself how hard he's working for Kosen-rufu, for society and for his members' development. With this yardstick, you can gauge a person's value, whereas your own personal sentiments may blind you to his worth. Unless you view people in the light of their own objectives, you can't see their good qualities, and you'll overlook many capable people.

You can't become a good leader unless you can recognize people's strong points. First, resolve to develop this insight and second, polish your own mirror through faith. With the *Ichinen* to make another person happy, you will naturally discover his best qualities.

When you can't guide a person all by yourself, take him to one of your seniors whom he can get close to. Any small-mindedness on your part will prevent him from developing. The essence of guidance lies in enabling members to develop freely, taking into account the many methods available.

Watch out for your own likes and dislikes in judging others, and never regard a person as your subordinate. Quietly observe his personality, popularity and character with an objective eye.

Understanding another person is not easy, but when you polish the mirror of your faith by chanting Daimoku, you can perceive his essential nature.

Like the proverb, "You can't see the forest for the trees," when you're overwhelmed by a busy schedule, you can't judge things objectively.

By taking a higher, broader view based on the *Gosho* and the practice of Buddhism, you can see everything from a clear perspective.

Wisdom and good fortune

What difference is there between Gakkai members and others, when both are human beings and members of society? The difference is in terms of true, eternal good fortune.

Without true faith, successful businessmen and other affluent people only grasp after fleeting joys. They have a kind of fortune, but according to Buddhism, it belongs to the world of *rapture* and is limited to this life only. Their whole lives are as transient as a stage play or foam on the water's surface. This is the fundamental difference between those who practice Buddhism and others.

A person who practices the life-philosophy of Nichiren Daishonin and makes it his foundation will develop a correct view of life. He is like a massive, deeply-rooted tree; nothing can topple him, no matter what happens.

Others in society may seem happy, from the outside, but the roots of their fortune are shallow, and a strong wind will bring them crashing down. Even when the outward appearance is similar, there is a vast, intrinsic difference between their happiness and ours.

Generally speaking, some people have fortune while others have wisdom. There are professors of economics whose poverty forces them to frequent pawn shops. Men of high intelligence don't necessarily have fortune. On the other hand, there are uneducated people who successfully develop their own enterprises. They have good fortune.

Those who embrace the Gohonzon acquire both good fortune and wisdom to establish absolute happiness. A passage from the *Ongi Kuden* reads, *All things in the universe inherently possess immeasurable wisdom and fortune. Nam-myoho-renge-kyo provides both wisdom and fortune.* From a broader viewpoint, those who enjoy good fortune now must have praised the Gohonzon in the past.

Capable men

A stanza from an old Japanese song goes, "People are the walls of the castle and the castle itself." Capable people are absolutely essential in any field of society. Their presence is the most vital condition for achieving a great success.

You may raise capable people, but it is also important to find them. By taking leadership with faith as your basis and cherishing the great objective of Kosen-rufu, you can evaluate people correctly. You can tell who's dedicated, who's sharp, who's sincere and so on.

Sometimes you can find a capable person intuitively in a moment, but at other times you can't judge someone's value until you've known him a long time. As a leader, your strong sense of responsibility and *Ichinen* to complete Kosen-rufu will enable you to discover and raise capable people.

All who embrace the Gohonzon are potentially capable. Grass, trees and flowers appear in the world to benefit man in one way or another. Their use depends on the wisdom of men.

Similarly, the proper use of people depends on the leader's concern for society, true Buddhism and Kosen-rufu. Master the art of enabling every member to give his best.

Putting a capable person in the wrong place can paralyze the whole organization and ruin other capable people.

Insofar as you dislike being advised or are surrounded by those who only compliment you, you can never find capable people.

Raising capable leaders

There are some basic principles for raising leaders.

First of all, give those whom you feel are potential leaders a chance to develop. Even if you feel somewhat hesitant about their qualifications, let them try to show results.

⚜

Secondly, use your own experiences in life to develop your ability in giving guidance. Sometimes you'll need to give dynamic, inspiring guidance and at other times, detailed instruction. With faith as your basis, perfect your ability to give guidance as an example for your juniors.

⚜

Thirdly, have them study the life-philosophy of Nichiren Daishonin. No matter how enthusiastic one may be, without a theoretical grasp of Buddhism, he'll lose confidence when he confronts a serious situation or meets *Sansho Shima*. A thorough knowledge of Buddhism will also enable one to convince others to practice. Without this knowledge, he cannot be an effective leader, either in the organization or in society.

Lastly, personality is very important. You should raise people who will be reliable. A sincere individual wins the trust of others and is qualified as a leader. However, you cannot judge a person by his appearance alone. Ultimately, those who are sincere and consistent will prove to be capable individuals.

Training your juniors

You yourself will develop when you strive to help your juniors grow. Leaders should never be passive. Former President Toda fervently hoped that through his guidance, his members would grow to surpass him. This is a leader's ultimate desire.

The Sokagakkai is steadily developing without a moment's interruption, just as the earth never stops rotating, and cells never stop dividing. Leaders must always develop themselves; otherwise they cannot train their juniors.

In every campaign, take the initiative to discover and train people to become future leaders. This is *Hon'in-myo*, the cause for victory and dynamic growth into the the limitless future.

☙

Developing capable people means raising leaders with strong faith. To accomplish this, you must teach them the Gakkai spirit, to conquer all *Sansho Shima* and maintain firm faith in the Gohonzon till the end. Then, put them in a position where they can freely utilize their maximum ability.

☙

It is wrong to say that so-and-so is "no good." In certain aspects he definitely surpasses you, and you should help him develop those strong points. This is the fundamental spirit of training capable people.

Encouragement and self-awakening

Two plants of the same kind grow at a remarkably different rate when one is planted in a sunny place and the other in the shade. In the same way, leaders will develop when they are given timely encouragement, but they won't without receiving the proper guidance. Of course, one's own self-awakening comes first; unless he wants to develop, guidance is useless. Development itself, however, results from thorough, appropriate guidance. One who merely waits for capable people to appear is not a leader.

Training, protection, guidance and teaching

In Buddhism there is the principle of *Kyo Chi Gyo I*. *Kyo* and *Chi* together indicate faith. *Gyo* means action and *I* position. A leader's activities and responsibility must be consistent with his position in the organization.

Unless a leader strives to fulfill his position, according to the principle of *Ninpo Ikka*, he will hinder the organization's advancement. Even though each of us is still immature, the Daishonin teaches us to encourage each other and, through unity, to fulfill our mission.

If a member has a problem, guide him kindly so that he won't come to a standstill. When he is tired after strenuous activities, you should protect him. If he doesn't understand the Gakkai spirit, train him. If he raises a question about the life-philosophy of Nichiren Daishonin, you should teach him. Become the kind of leader people trust because they gain confidence and find solutions to their problems when they talk to you.

Some people may stop practicing if you train them when you should be protecting them. On the other hand, you may spoil members by being easy with them when they require training. Being able to give appropriate guidance is part of a leader's capability.

It is vital to encourage your junior members kindly and talk with them as though they were your own brothers and sisters. In addition, you should realize how fortunate you are to be able to explain even a little about Buddhism to others, and resolve to help them develop.

Faith and weakness

What never changes throughout one's three existences of life is called nature, or Sho. Sometimes we have to observe a person's background and history in order to know his true nature. His inherent weaknesses will remain dormant and not hinder him so long as he is devoted to his practice and follows his seniors with a determination to grow.

However, if he is satisfied and relaxes, all his negative karma from the past will definitely emerge. Remember this point both in observing others and in reflecting on yourself.

Developing capable people

The important thing in life is confidence. Don't be a weak leader who gets discouraged when one of your members moves away to take a new job. You should be proud of sending him to another location where he can become a fine leader someday.

What counts is raising leaders who can work for society and for Kosen-rufu. Being narrow-minded, self-deprecating or lacking in self-confidence simply reflects your weak *Ichinen* or conviction. Think positively and advance with confidence.

Believers in the Gohonzon, whatever their

field of endeavor, each have some specific mission. You can accumulate fortune when you're convinced of your mission.

Youth division leaders

The spirit of youth division leaders has been described in specific guidances for youth. All you have to do is to put it into practice. As for concrete problems, you should consult your senior leaders and try to pick up their rhythm.

Leaders' responsibilities and the kind of guidance they give will differ according to their position. The basic thing is to take good care of the youth division. Don't act out of formality simply because you have a position, and never become authoritarian.

The Gakkai world should have a spirited atmosphere, but don't be swayed by your emotions when giving guidance. Though you may be resented, keep cool and refrain from impulsiveness.

As a humanistic leader, you should make friends with your youth division members and be on good terms with them. The basis of leadership is faith in the Gohonzon and humanism.

Just because you become a youth division leader, don't think you have to wear fine clothes or put on airs. By all means, never be authoritarian or formal. As a passage from the *Gosho* reads, *The higher the teaching (one cherishes), the lower the position (he takes).* Join in with your members and lead them with conviction and broad-mindedness. That's the spirit of a true leader.

Be a young revolutionary who can fight at a crucial moment. Be a youth division leader who can use good judgment and protect Buddhism, with the courage to crush evil and promote justice.

To inspire a vibrant spirit in your group, you, as the leader, must first stand alone. If you chant Daimoku to the Gohonzon for your members' development, your wish will penetrate their lives.

When you, as a youth division leader, practice without restraint, your members will naturally change. Buddhism terms this consistency from beginning to end *(Honmatsu Kukyo-to)*.

When it comes to basic matters of Buddhism, speak out straightforwardly, according to the teachings of former President Toda. This is faith. When members have specific problems, guide them with a readiness to practice right along with them.

A youth division leader disqualifies himself as a true revolutionary if he pretends excellence as a leader, feels obligated to make eloquent speeches or makes it appear that he knows everything about Buddhism. He will only suffer if he does so.

Dignity

One who can calmly and imperturbably handle a crisis or confront the three strong enemies *(Sanrui-no Goteki)* is a man of dignity.

You are not qualified to be a leader if you are swayed by such problems. Tell the members firmly, "Don't worry. We can change poison into medicine, can't we? This is all happening exactly as the Daishonin said it would, so there's nothing to get upset about." Take a broad view of the situation from the standpoint of faith and guide the members accordingly. Seeing your air of calm dignity, they'll feel reassured and take courage.

An individual of dignity can confidently Shakubuku anyone, even a famous personality or someone with high social standing. He can convincingly assert his views on current affairs and life-philosophy.

Some leaders within our organization might appear important, but unless they are equally valued in society, they do not have true dignity. A dictionary calls it, "The quality or state of being worthy."

All phenomena are part of Buddhism. One who takes leadership in life based on this conviction is a great hero and a man of dignity.

Dignity and generosity

Dignity and generosity are essential to a leader. Dignity is faith. Generosity is the sincere feeling with which leaders think of individual members.

Opinions

Opinions can be classified as either living opinions or dead opinions. Living opinions are not bound by personal bias, but take the whole group into consideration. They embody the spirit of cooperation, can be readily put into practice and are constructive. On the contrary, dead opinions are damaging, oppressive, complaining, or they are taken as sarcasm. Dead opinions are destructive.

Living opinions are attractive, give people a good feeling and make them want to cooperate. This is the kind of opinion which befits a leader.

Development

Even those who worry about not having the ability to give guidance can master it naturally as they continue to chant Daimoku. Although your own ability may be limited, if you have a strong *Ichinen* for your members to become capable people and even surpass you, that alone will definitely enable you to get good results. This is in keeping with a quotation from the Sutra, "We have obtained a priceless gem without seeking it."

Although you are told, "Develop the ability to give guidance," you cannot do it in a day. Faith would be unnecessary if you could change yourself through words alone. People have studied books on moral discipline since the beginning of history. If it were all that simple, everyone would have long since developed a perfect character and we'd have a happier world than we do today.

Man's destiny ordinarily limits the extent to which he can improve himself. Only with the supreme Law as the basis can he transform his destiny and achieve his human revolution. One may, through moral discipline, realize his faults and even temporarily hold them in check. However, this is not a fundamental change. When you chant Daimoku, you can attain your human revolution naturally.

It is ideal for youth to have power, good judgment and broad minds, but they need not have all three. Youth are still in the making, and a promising future lies ahead. Plunge ahead with courage and passion and don't worry about your shortcomings.

If people respect and trust you just by looking at you, this is guidance without words. The ability to give guidance comes from your prayers that your members will have stronger faith and become happier, and that you yourself will fulfill your responsibilities. Talent and strategy are not the essence of the real ability to give guidance.

Leading the way

The principle of guidance is basic to the Sokagakkai. Guidance is leading members to the Gohonzon, saying, "Let's chant Daimoku." It is of secondary importance to explain what the Gohonzon is. Guidance means to lead people to chant Daimoku and to participate in specific Gakkai activities.

Suppose a member asks you a question. You can guide him even though you do not know the answer. You can say, "Let's go ask another leader who can answer your question." This is good guidance. Don't get caught up in merely teaching members from A to Z by yourself. Leading the way has far more value, as it forestalls stalemate and opens the way to limitless growth.

Teaching others while pretending to have knowledge is a form of hypocrisy and inevitably leads to a deadlock. Our basic approach is guidance. Sometimes, of course, we also need to teach, train or protect the members. The principle of guidance includes all of these elements.

※ ※ ※

If you forget the spirit of guidance, you will be side-tracked by your emotions or become authoritarian. Mercy should always underlie guidance. It's cowardly to avoid your responsibility by leaving a person's problem up to another leader without making an effort to help solve it.

※ ※ ※

Don't feel hesitant when you give guidance. Frankly tell people about your fervent conviction toward Kosen-rufu. Warmly encourage them by relating your own experiences. Youthful guidance with a sense of freshness and originality is important. Disregard formality, keep abreast of the times and give guidance with true Buddhism as the basis.

When you go to an outlying area on a guidance tour, you should give full consideration to the future development of that locale. Your unwise leadership and self-satisfied attitude become obvious if your guidance is geared only to fit the occasion. Neither should your guidance be overly influenced by the schedule prepared by local leaders. From a perspective broader than their own, you should be able to drive home the wedge for the future development of each locale you visit.

Compassion is important in giving guidance. You're to blame, though, if you don't say what you should. Your strict guidance can be the cause of a member's great development. When leaders give guidance in high spirits, their members will also become high-spirited. This is in keeping with the principles of the fusion of subject and object *(Kyochi Myogo)* and the inseparability of a person and his environment *(Esho Funi)*.

Every guidance should be based on the conviction that it will awaken the member to faith and be the motivation for a lifelong practice.

Reporting

There are two kinds of reports. One can be understood as it stands, but the other cannot be taken at face value. A report will vary according to the character of the person who is giving it. Some people are apt to underestimate things, while others overestimate things and still others are easily deceived. Therefore, you should first of all judge the character of the person who makes the report.

The way someone views a situation changes according to his mental and physical condition. For this reason, you may misjudge a matter if you fail to perceive the inner state or real motivation of the person reporting. A leader should master the ability to draw accurate conclusions upon seeing someone or hearing him report.

Our organization deals with human lives, which are infinitely precious, yet some leaders still forget to communicate with or to contact others, or remain in the dark about matters they should fully understand. This is proof that they lack mercy.

Buddha means *Hoshin Nyorai,* a person of wisdom. The function of Buddha is mercy. Some leaders forget such crucial points because they don't use good judgment or because they're inconsiderate. As they develop their faith, however, they will be able to fulfill all their responsibilities successfully.

※

Don't always expect good reports. Always be ready to receive unfavorable reports. Good reports present no need for worry, but bad reports demand your full attention and require immediate action. In such cases, a leader must be capable of judging whether a report has been made conscientiously or not.

※

The first thing to remember is to report facts just as they are. What's more, don't think your own responsibility is over just because you make a report. Leaders should have the conviction to guide members on the spot and resolve any problem.

You should be able to report the number of people present when you attend a meeting, regardless of how many there are. Leaders cannot become great if they're unaware of the presence of troublemakers or shirk their responsibility, thinking that someone else will take care of it. Responsibility is hard, but you can only develop yourself when you're determined to take it on.

Forbearance

The "robe of gentleness and forbearance" mentioned in the Lotus Sutra means mercy and broad-mindedness. When you hear that someone is about to stop practicing, you cannot help him if you get emotional or feel contempt for him. That will make him quit for sure. Persevere with him in every possible way. Have this determination: "I've got to help him practice." This attitude will be your "robe of gentleness and forbearance."

Some non-members may slander our organization. You should realize how unhappy they are and remember that unless you Shakubuku them, they may remain miserable throughout their lives. Resolve to convince these people of Buddhism's validity and bring them to a discussion meeting.

This attitude is also "donning the robe of gentleness and forbearance."

General of generals

If a general is not wise, his soldiers will be unhappy. Excellent aides may assist the unwise general, but their efforts will be in vain. A good example is Chu Ke Kung Ming[1] who, after the death of his master Liu Pei Hsuan Tei, served the master's son, Liu Chen. A good general must always be thinking of concrete directions to give those who come to him seeking guidance.

When someone doesn't follow your instructions, you should still show him respect. Only when you continue to respect him, will he listen to you and come to respect you in turn. Don't avoid those who put forth opinions.

Never let your immediate juniors become conceited. The closer they are to you, the more severe you should be with them. This is the way

---

[1] Chu Ke Kung Ming (181-234)—strategist and statesman; helped Liu Pei Hsuan Tei establish the kingdom of Shu. After his lord's death, he supported his incompetent son, though urged to rule himself to preserve the state.

to develop your junior members successfully.

Assistance

When you accompany members to help them do Shakubuku in an outlying area, they will not be pleased or trust you unless you produce results. You have failed miserably if your hosts think of you as a nuisance. In assisting members in Shakubuku, warmly support their leader and make them all stand up with confidence.

Even when it is your help that achieves successful results, give full credit to the local leaders. The organization won't function through strategy alone. Only when an individual exercises his full potential as a leader will the organization move.

Everything depends on the leader's willingness to fight. Tactics have little to do with faith. A leader should take charge of an inactive district and make it prosper by personally encouraging the members and setting an example through his own practice of Buddhism.

At the same time, a visiting leader should not be swayed by a single district alone. He should maintain a view of the whole, exercising reserve and confidence in leadership. Though a leader may devote himself diligently to a given area, the organization as a whole will be weakened if he fails to see the broader aspects.

On the frontline of activities

Leaders should always fight on the frontline of activities, side by side with their members, and then return to take care of matters within the organization. This is necessary in order to lead the whole group. They cannot take true leadership unless they move constantly between frontline activities and behind-the-scenes guidance for the campaign. Leaders should take the lead on the front lines, guiding the members with the example of their own practice.

When giving guidance, be determined that the activities you lead will create the history of Kosen-rufu. That way you can fulfill your mission as a leader. Never be swayed by the force of habit.

A great leader must be wise, and when giving guidance, he should also be passionate.

Once you stand up, everyone else will, too. You should create unity among the members, based on this confidence.

The leaders are the nucleus of the organization. The nucleus in human society means unity. Tremendous power results when the nucleus of unity explodes into action. The power of faith enables you to enjoy yourself even during the struggle of a hard campaign. This joy shows that you are accumulating great fortune and bringing about deep change in your karma.

Completing formalities is not everything. Former President Toda often said, "The headquarters is wherever the President is," and would not allow us to build a headquarters building for a long time.

Initiative

It is a leader's responsibility to give deep, thorough consideration as to how the organization is to advance.

Achieving a goal requires painstaking preparation. Your plans should be original and enable the whole group to advance. Plans are not made for formality's sake but in order to create value.

Whenever you see someone, give him a dream for the future. Especially with young people, you should inspire hope and show them a glorious vision. Otherwise you cannot be called a true leader.

Leadership and the law of Kyochi

From the viewpoint of *Kyochi,* if leaders *(chi)* have capability, confidence and wisdom, their members *(kyo)* will also develop confidence and strength. If leaders speak only in line of duty and without feeling, their listeners will be bored. If leaders assume a businesslike attitude, they will produce only businesslike members.

Official and personal matters

Former President Toda would tell us, "Don't listen to your wife, but listen to her." He meant that we should never listen to our wives concerning official affairs of the organization, but pay attention to what they say about personal matters. The successful resolving of personal affairs and the promotion of Kosen-rufu require decisions made and put into practice on the basis of our self-awakening and sense of responsibility. A chief should consult with his assistants. This is essential to making decisions. For example, a chapter chief should consult with the district chiefs, who practice closely together with him.

Even if a chapter chief's wife is the chapter women's leader, he should not be swayed by her. He should be impartial and draw a strict line between official and personal affairs; otherwise, she will lead the chapter. This is the way of a true leader. The strength of our organization lies in the strict distinction between official and personal matters.

You should listen to your wife because she worries about you and heed her advice concerning personal matters and affairs close to you. But pay no attention when she speaks ill of others or informs you of a rumor.

Changing poison into medicine

Faith means changing any problem into a benefit through the principle of *Hendoku Iyaku*. Guide your juniors with the confidence that you will definitely make them happy.

We use an air-conditioner on hot days and a heater on cold days. All sorts of obstacles will arise on the road to Kosen-rufu. Leaders take the role of an air-conditioner in the summer or a heater in the winter, solving their members' problems and making them happy.

Dismissals

We sometimes remove a leader from his position after carefully considering his situation, in order to help him re-establish his faith and his daily life. If he holds a grudge because of his dismissal, it shows arrogance and vanity on his part. This is the same life-condition as that of Daibadatta. From another viewpoint, his dismissal stems from his inclination towards resentment.

You don't really know yourself. It's human to attribute our faults to others. It is vital to give deeply considerate guidance when you dismiss a leader. Dismissals are far more difficult than appointments.

In dismissing a leader, unless he has betrayed the organization or stopped practicing, give him encouragement and instructions which will enable him to firmly establish his faith. Encouragement is the best guidance. By all means, avoid treating a dismissal in a cold or bureaucratic manner.

The most important things in an organization are personnel and financial affairs. A failure in either will destroy any group, even a family. The loss of a strict, impartial attitude in personnel or financial affairs will create a deadlock and ruin the organization.

When one of your members is dismissed, you may reflect on your own shortcomings as a leader in guiding him, but don't think of it solely as your fault. Nichiren Daishonin appointed six main priests. However, after the Daishonin passed away, five of them turned against him. In this case, it was not the Daishonin, but the five priests who were to blame.

In dismissing a group chief, for example, encourage him to continue his faith so that he can soon regain that responsibility or surpass it.

Never discourage people

In guiding members, you should never say, "That's no good." What they want to hear is a concrete method of solving the problem, not your negative evaluation. A good leader is one who can give his members confidence and a clear direction.

For example, when a member tells you, "My guest wouldn't join tonight," encourage him by saying, "I've had the same experience more times than you. Don't worry, you tried your best, so you'll definitely get benefits."

However, you should firmly protest unjust or misleading philosophies which slander the Sokagakkai. Don't back down a single step. But when it comes to the members who are fighting together for Kosen-rufu, you should always encourage them warmly.

Fairness and generosity

A leader must not be influenced by his personal feelings. When he observes his members calmly, he can understand their character and personality.

※

It's important to put the right man in the right place. Never decide personnel affairs on the basis of groundless suspicions, guesswork or your own personal likes and dislikes. On the basis of faith, you should consider how one can most effectively contribute toward Kosen-rufu.

※

"It is easy to become a general of soldiers; it is hard to become the general of generals." Develop the magnanimity and leadership abilities to enable any person to work for Kosen-rufu.

※

If you know someone's strong points and weak points, trust him deeply and instruct him well; then he will surely follow you.

The proper attitude in giving guidance may be expressed in one word: sincerity. You need a sincere and passionate determination to make someone happy or to help him understand even a little about Nichiren Daishonin's life-philosophy. It has nothing to do with whether or not you're a good speaker. With the sincerity that comes through faith, you will naturally develop the wisdom to give the most suitable guidance. This is the principle of attaining *enlightenment* through faith *(Ishin Tokunyu).*

Leaders must always be considerate. Unless they think of the whole, the general members will suffer.

Based on the principle of democracy, you should take good care of the people who are working hard and carrying out their responsibilities. Where management is not considerate, workers are miserable. It is a mistake to think you can buy people's effort just by raising their wages. What counts is understanding.

Herein lies the basic principle of Buddhist democracy.

The human mind

It's never difficult to understand the inner workings of a person's mind. For example, you should be able to answer to yourself, "Is he very tired?" "Is he doing his best?" or "What is he seeking?"

※

You'll never understand people if you force your opinions on them without paying attention to their views, or if you try to judge them solely on the basis of your own limited experience. You can understand their true feelings when you're sincerely concerned for them. For example, it's useless to ask someone to study if he's too tired. You must get to know the human mind.

It is essential to understand what a person needs to be happy.

※

The cause of your worries is simpler than you think. For example, if leaders make a schedule and let members know it in advance, everyone can act with reassurance. If leaders are too lazy to do this, they'll cause trouble for many people.

You must be very careful. The meeting of the planning board is held in a strict manner to discuss even small particulars, and this is important. Even if you think a problem is trivial, it could be a major problem for the general members. You should know this much about people's minds.

Leaders should be composed, prudent and, when the occasion is right, take decisive leadership. The members will miss their chance to fight if a leader is indecisive or leaves ambiguous what should be made clear. Unless you can warmly raise your junior members, you will not be protected.

You should, by all means, keep your promises and be prompt. Don't keep people waiting. Otherwise you will betray their trust and make them turn away from you. If the meeting time is inconvenient for you or if some urgent business arises, be sure to communicate and send someone in your place. Then the people who come to the meeting can go home feeling satisfied. If you can't do that, you are lacking in mercy and have essentially disqualified yourself as a leader.

As a leader, never think you are great. Members are following the Gohonzon, not you. You're conceited if you think that they practice because you're special.

I sometimes scold the leaders, but you shouldn't imitate me only out of formality. My purpose in scolding is to destroy the devil in their minds. Therefore, you should not follow me in form and language alone. It is important to encourage the members in all sincerity.

Sincerity is also the basic point in giving guidance to members who are older than you. In one sense, you need to show them respect. However, in matters of faith you should maintain a firm attitude.

When a member sets out on a campaign, it is important to answer immediately, "All right. Do your best." If you don't, your junior members will lose enthusiasm. Even a short word will encourage them tremendously.

When the campaign schedule is so pressing that members don't even seem to have time to eat, they cannot take capable leadership. When you're aware of whether the members present are hungry or tired and guide them accordingly, you have grasped the spirit of the *Gosho, On the Selection of Time (Senji Sho)*.

Leaders should always think of their members and be constantly asking if this district is all right, or if that chapter is doing well. This is called "Maiji sa ze nen" in the Sutra, and it means "I am always thinking of this." The groups for which a leader is responsible will develop only through his *Ichinen*.

Criticism

Don't get nervous or be influenced by criticism of our organization. To begin with, listening to such criticism will not make you happy. It's important to be aware of people's feelings in your own social circles, but you needn't overly concern yourself about criticism of our organization. The Sokagakkai has grown to what it is today even in the midst of criticism. We should follow the principle of *Zuijii*, not of *Zuitai*.

Those who turn a deaf ear to outside static and advance with conviction are true pioneers. They will surely be victorious in the end.

Master the Gakkai spirit

Even if you worship the Gohonzon, you cannot do Shakubuku, receive benefits or feel joyful unless you follow the right person *(Zenchishiki*, or good leader). This is the amazing thing about our organization, which is based on the living principle of faith. When you follow this principle, you will gain wisdom, benefits and confidence, and people will follow you naturally.

To become a leader, you must master the Gakkai spirit. All people are in essence "Buddhas," which is an eternal and natural condition of life. It is the way of Buddhism to fully realize this potential *(Jitai Kensho)*. Stay close to your senior leaders and don't hesitate or retreat a single step.

Planning and action

When you take action, set a goal and map

out a plan. However, life never goes exactly as planned.

Even in battle, it's not unusual to advance, thinking, "The enemy's over there," only to discover that the enemy is actually behind you.

Planning is like a strategical map or knowledge put onto paper. Daily life and activities involve the practical application of knowledge. It's vital to use good judgment according to the circumstances *(Zuien Shinnyo-no Chi)*.

Government offices devoted solely to planning do, in fact, cause many failures. When emergency measures are conducted in accordance with *Zuien Shinnyo-no Chi*, they will be more effective. If everything went exactly as planned, every single organization and business would succeed.

In carrying out our campaign, it's important to make a plan and put it into practice, experiencing trials and errors until you can match theory with reality.

Concrete guidelines

Guidance, whether given individually or at discussion meetings, should be concrete. When a member has specific questions, you can deeply encourage him by simply relating your own experiences. Leaders should always create a bright atmosphere. Consider the needs of each person attending, and give convincing guidance that will stir deep emotion and confidence in your listeners.

If a leader tells the same story at every meeting, the participants get bored and are forced to endure it with feigned interest. This is a defeat on the leader's part. If he frankly shares his own experience in a lively yet friendly way, he will move people and leave them with a lasting impression.

Law and person

When you receive guidance, make the determination that within a year or two, you will develop the same Gakkai spirit as your leader. Those who have this strong seeking mind will eventually become winners in society. Members who make a direct connection with their seniors will definitely gain. We owe what we are now to the discipline, training and encouragement we have received from our senior leaders.

Law is ultimately equivalent to Person. This principle is revealed in the *Gosho, On the True Object of Worship (Kanjin-no Honzon Sho)*. There is no other way to put it into practice than to follow the organization and receive guidance from your senior leaders.

Faith and position

One's position in the organization does not indicate the degree of his faith. You're mistaken if you think someone has deep faith just because he becomes a leader. Faith is a matter of being strict with yourself.

This is explained in the *Gosho: Even if you may become wise and learned, what use will it be if you fall into hell?*

When your members have questions, you can guide them warmly and courageously so long as you yourself are developing. On the other hand, if you are not developing, you will be swayed by your personal feelings and provoke antagonism from people who would otherwise understand your guidance quite easily.

What is the source of development? First, it is the power of Daimoku. Second, it's doing your best in your work and in carrying out your responsibilities. Third is your moment-to-moment determination, which gives rise to delight, hope and the driving force of progress.

If your friend, whom you've worked together with in Gakkai campaigns is appointed to a higher position, you should feel glad for him. If you become jealous or hold a grudge against him, consider it your own shame.

The purpose of faith is not to obtain a position, but to attain *enlightenment.* Don't deprecate yourself too much. The fundamental question, even for directors and the President, is how much one will do for Buddhism, how much fortune he can accumulate and whether he'll be able to enjoy life to the fullest *(Shujo Sho Yuraku).*

Faith is not formality. It's ridiculous to expect people to respect you just because you're a chapter or district leader.

A true leader is someone whom others continue to respect even when he's relieved of his position, saying, "His faith is beautiful. As a Gakkai member he is a true leader." It's frightening that some people chase after illusions in their eagerness for a position.

Heroes of this age

Someone said that a hero in this age is one who appears from among the people and unites the efforts of all. This is a correct idea.

In the end, everything depends on human beings. There are no perfect beings or supermen. From now on especially, it is more important to harmonize the capabilities of many different people than to rely on the talent of a single outstanding individual.

The *Gosho* states, *Buddha is called a worldly hero.* Since we are following the will of Nichiren Daishonin, the True Buddha, we do the work of the Buddha in this world. Therefore, the name "worldly hero." Leaders who, with Buddhism as their basis, have confidence in giving and carrying out instructions and motivating people in Gakkai activities are "worldly heroes."

Self-confidence

Some people say they have no self-confidence, but all they need do is be themselves. You don't have to chant Daimoku loudly to receive benefits. It's fine to chant in a calm voice if your heart is brimming with confidence. If you imitate others, you will lose your own characteristics and become a person of half measure. Cherry blossoms are only cherry blossoms, and chrysanthemums are nothing but chrysanthemums.

You may temporarily lose your self-confidence when scolded by a leader. However, when you regain it, that will be real self-confidence. Genuine self-confidence will not give way to reprimand.

Communication

A proverb goes, "Silence is golden." However, it is wrong. Those who remain silent may be crafty, but leaders are valuable because they speak out. It is a Confucian idea to utter one word only after thinking nine times. It is the principle of democracy to speak, write, read and advance.

The second high priest, Nikko Shonin, left Twenty-six Warning Articles. One of them reads, "You should delight in discussions and lectures on Buddhism but do not pass the time in idle conversation." To "delight in discussions and lectures on Buddhism" means discussion, lectures and Shakubuku for the sake of Kosen-rufu.

People do not develop through general guidance alone. You should repeatedly have person-to-person talks. Both individual and general guidance are needed to achieve success.

There should be an atmosphere of lively talk wherever members gather. Otherwise there can be no development. A cheerful atmosphere in which leaders can speak freely indicates growth. A dull meeting with no lively conversation is a sign of regression.

Body and function

In dealing with any problem, it is wise to adapt yourself to the circumstances. Life is an eternal struggle for existence. You must decide how to handle changing circumstances case by case. Basically, you should have the spirit to achieve Kosen-rufu no matter what, and not be swayed by either praise or criticism. Nothing will ever sway me from my objective. I am not in the least influenced by praise or censure. All I have to do is to achieve Kosen-rufu.

According to the principle of *Kutai Kuyu*, each member of the organization has a unique role and should therefore strive to the utmost in his particular situation. The Gohonzon is the absolute "body" *(tai)* and as members, we serve as the "function" *(yu)*. As for the Sokagakkai, the President is "body" and its leaders are the "function." In a chapter, the chapter chief is the "body" and the district leaders are the "function."

The world of Buddhism

Leaders should always appear as bright as the morning sun. You should not work reluctantly just because you're told to. Do everything voluntarily for your own sake. This is faith.

Leaders should keep in close contact with their juniors. Don't avoid their doubts or questions, but tackle them without hesitation. Put your understanding into full use to answer your members' questions, and solve their problems as though you were cutting tangled knots with a sharp sword.

Outside of the Sokagakkai, people often utter honeyed words while inwardly preoccupied with selfish interests. Many think of nothing but cheating others. Because our organization is the world of Buddhism, we can speak out frankly about anything. Sometimes our words may hurt other members' feelings, but fundamentally we speak for the sake of Buddhism.

A swan seems to glide along calmly, but under the water, where no one can see, it paddles furiously. Leaders are like the swan's webbed feet. Only through their strenuous efforts behind the scenes can the whole organization advance with reassurance.

Chapter Two: Ichinen

Ichinen

A passage from the *Gosho* reads, *If you think the Law is outside yourself, it is not the supreme Law (Myoho). Ichinen* is a matter of faith. Nothing is stronger than the *Ichinen* of faith, the power developed through practice. Nichiren Daishonin states, *One's Ichinen when chanting Nam-myoho-renge-kyo permeates the entire universe. It can move anything.*

The *Maka* of *Maka Shikan* means great, and *Shikan*, to focus one's mind and realize the Buddha's wisdom. From the viewpoint of Nichiren Daishonin's Buddhism, it means to focus your *Ichinen* on chanting Daimoku to the Gohonzon and bring out the world of *enlightenment* from within your own life. This is the true meaning of *Maka Shikan*. Your strong prayers, not formality, will arouse the supreme Law.

A leader's determination

Everything depends on a leader's determination to make each of his members happy. His Daimoku for their happiness will effect a change "from poison to medicine," even if a member has an accident.

A leader should put his members' happiness before everything. Then his determination will touch their lives. This mirrors the Buddhist principles of consistency from beginning to end *(Honmatsu Kukyo-to)* and the inseparability of man and his environment *(Esho Funi)*.

A passage from the *Gosho* reads, *If a tree is deeply rooted, its branches spread wide. If a river starts deep in the mountains, its stream will be long.* The faith of leaders is the foundation of everything. When the leaders maintain a strong practice, the members will have no worries. So long as leaders individually determine to shoulder responsibility for the Sokagakkai, become friends with each other and create unity, the organization will never be destroyed.

Authoritarianism

Lead by example; do everything yourself first. It is cheap and underhanded to order others around. A good leader can warmly say, when unable to attend a meeting, "Sorry I can't go this evening, but will you please handle the meeting and encourage everyone?" Authoritarianism has absolutely no place in our organization.

The foundation for victory

Unflagging, day-by-day efforts in Shakubuku and personal guidance are the source of victory.

A journey of a thousand miles begins with one step. Minute drops of water make up the great ocean. Our victory to date is the result of each individual's thorough, untiring practice.

Just as one wave, another, then thousands upon thousands of waves will eventually wear away rocks, our activities, slowly but surely, are building a foundation for victory among the people.

Bonds of affection

Life-to-life bonds among members constitute *Itai Doshin*. The President must protect the general members, and senior members must protect their juniors, not superficially, but with a sense of absolute responsibility. Gakkai members, regardless of their position, are striving together to build a new society under the protection of the Gohonzon. Their bonds of friendship should never be broken.

In other organizations, seniors are often arrogant in teacher-pupil, employer-employee or senior-junior relationships. This is wrong. In the Sokagakkai, everything depends on faith. At times, a junior member spurs his senior on to greater efforts.

As leaders, we must remember to protect each other and never forget our bonds as fellow disciples.

If you try to lead others without developing yourself, you will be drawn off course. Everything will feel heavy to you. The fundamental point is your own development.

Another important thing is to be yourself. Each person has his own character and personality; therefore, if you speak from your own heart with the Gohonzon as your basis, you can guide your members easily and assuredly.

Resolution

Carry through what you've decided to do. One's behavior reflects his faith *(Gyotai soku Shinjin),* so fulfilling your resolution is the Buddhist practice. By so doing, you can achieve your human revolution.

Determine to carry out your resolution no matter how long it takes. If you can't do it in one month, do it in two months or three. This *Ichinen* will strengthen the very core of your life, the entity of *Ichinen Sanzen.*

Carry out whatever you've promised to the Gohonzon as well as your resolution for lifelong practice *(Issho Jobutsu).* Only then will you perfect your life. Fulfilling determinations spells growth and taps the source of great benefit.

Don't get upset just because a member has a problem. That's why you're there as a leader. Take time to tackle problems and solve them one by one. Where there are people, there are problems. A leader should realize that there will always be problems and resolve to handle them all with the Gohonzon as the basis.

Self-development

In order for everyone to move ahead happily, you yourself must advance happily first. Because people and their environment are inseparable *(Esho Funi)*, those around you will mirror your cheerful attitude.

However, this requires that you take the initiative, chant Daimoku earnestly and strive to develop yourself. There is no other way. This is no different from preparing yourself to give guidance or to lecture. Naturally, you should study the material and digest it ahead of your members in order to feel confident and at ease.

New era

The public has been amazed by the feeling they sense from our cultural activities such as the Fife and Drum Corps. They are surprised that the Sokagakkai has such a modern spirit. From now on, in order to be effective, leaders will need a fresh sense of the times.

Don't think that a capable man with strong faith is someone who keeps people waiting or who assembles them simply to hear him talk. You should be on the move, taking prompt, voluntary and appropriate action based on correct judgment.

Everyone should be moved by your meetings and go home with a happy feeling. Otherwise, you don't deserve to be called a leader.

The times advance restlessly. You must study in order to keep up. Daimoku is the driving force of everything.

A leader's Ichinen

A country conducts its first nuclear test, and the whole world is thrown into fearful turmoil. Mankind dreads atomic power in the form of nuclear weapons, but when used for peaceful purposes, it will be of unprecedented value. Its use, for evil or good, depends entirely on the *Ichinen* of leaders.

Leaders must be humanistic, since their influence on the public is so great. Many more leaders are needed to help people become happy, which is why the Sokagakkai must raise capable individuals.

The lion king

So far as society is concerned, we should lead

lives as serene as warm spring weather. Within the organization, however, maintain strict faith, as uncompromising and severe as autumn frost. We must battle against the forces which cause people unhappiness, with the spirit of a lion king.

Gakkai spirit

After Nichiren Daishonin's death, Nikko Shonin, the second high priest, stood alone in carrying out his master's will. Because of his efforts, the pure lineage of Nichirenshoshu Buddhism has been correctly handed down to our generation. Our spirit should be the same as Nikko Shonin's.

When first President Tsunesaburo Makiguchi died, some members gave up their faith, some turned against the organization and others simply gave in to the dark trend of the times. Only former President Toda rose undauntedly to build the Sokagakkai. His spirit remains in our organization today.

As the scope of our activities broadens and our membership grows, this uncompromising tradition may be neglected. Yet the leaders of the organization must continue to uphold the Gakkai spirit—the spirit of former President Toda and Nikko Shonin.

Past and present

When all the leaders tackle their campaigns, earnestly considering the future of the Sokagakkai, that is Kosen-rufu and the lifelong practice for *enlightenment (Issho Jobutsu)*.

You may have won a hundred thousand campaigns in the past, but if you give up now, all your efforts will be meaningless. Even a million times zero equals zero. That's how strict Buddhism is.

Nichiro, one of the six elder priests who were disciples of Nichiren Daishonin, fought hard for Kosen-rufu. Today, however, he is considered a heretical priest, and all his accomplishments count for nothing because he abandoned faith after the Daishonin's death. Buddhism thus teaches us to keep faith until the last moment of our lives.

It is shallow and obsolete to think that leaders are appointed solely on the basis of their Shakubuku ability. Unless we carefully evaluate people's capabilities in giving guidance, carrying out activities, planning and so on from a long-range viewpoint, we cannot raise leaders for the new era.

※　※　※

The term *Gento* means present and future. President Toda once said, "*Gen* of *Gento* means master, while *to* indicates disciples." When leaders neglect their own progress, their members will suffer. In order to create a new era, each of us must become a capable leader who can keep abreast of the times.

※　※　※

Leave the past behind. You should advance with a strong *Ichinen* based on faith and develop into a new type of leader. Don't get puffed up about your past accomplishments. No matter how brilliant they were, the glory is fleeting. It is like one scene from a dream.

Now is the time to build a foundation for your development as a great leader who can meet the needs of the people.

※　※　※

Don't be caught up in the past. Become a

leader who will help materialize a new society filled with hope.

∽∽

Elderly people tend to cling to the past, but youth should live with the future in mind. "The two existences of present and future" *(Gento Nise)* means to aim toward the future from the basis of the present. With the spirit of *Gento Nise,* you can transform the past into the mainspring of a vibrant future. When it comes to faith, age makes no difference.

Praise and scolding

Basically, there are four types of people. Some individuals are spurred on to greater efforts and develop themselves when they are praised. Some grow from the experience of being praised at first and then scolded later on. A third group develops when they are scolded, while others are scolded and still don't grow. Few people develop just from being praised. You should be grateful and happy that there are people who take the trouble to scold you so that you can grow.

Scolding or reprimands from your leaders serve as the motivating power to change your destiny and also further your own development. It's your own devil-nature that makes you try to avoid being scolded. The spirit to go for guidance no matter what you're told shows a seeking mind.

Faith and hesitation

People try to defend themselves in order to justify their actions. While this may be understandable, a leader should not hesitate in pointing out where his juniors need to improve.

This kind of leader has mercy. When you frankly point out the problem spots in your members' practice, they can change their destiny and rid their lives of past negative causes. Be straightforward and tell them what you're really thinking.

When it comes to faith, hesitant or vague guidance will not help your members. The larger our organization grows, the more important direct, clear-cut guidance will become. Leaders must transmit to their members the tradition of strict guidance in faith, observed since the days of President Makiguchi and President Toda.

To advance joyfully with an open heart, you must chant Daimoku. When you chant sincerely, everything will open up for you. After giving someone strict guidance, chant for him: "Please, Gohonzon, he's got to understand!" When your members have problems, chant that they will solve them. This is the way leaders should practice.

Practice with absolute conviction, but use common sense when you talk to your members. When you must caution them, do so without hesitation, and when they need your support, encourage them right away. You don't need to do anything special. Just be yourself and talk with them in a way that's natural to you. If someone still quits, then it's his fault and not yours.

Expediency

Leaders must not be blindly influenced by the actions or opinions of others. They should advance on the basis of their own conviction — that is called *Zuijii*. In regard to Gakkai activities, expedient methods seldom work for long, nor do they necessarily produce real growth.

Surer methods might be more difficult, but your efforts will enable you to grow in faith. In order to solidify our organization, it is vital that leaders avoid an easy-going attitude or selfish expediency.

Crucial moments

The person who makes himself available at a crucial moment is a truly valuable individual. This is so in any sphere of activity — for example, the famed Minutemen of the American Revolution. But it is especially important in Buddhism and is the mark of true Gakkai spirit. Shijo Kingo rushed to his master's side to protect him during the Tatsunokuchi Persecution. His actions are an example for all Gakkai members.

Former President Toda once said, "One who will fight beside me at a crucial moment is a true disciple."

Relying on the force of numbers is cheap and cowardly, and from the standpoint of Buddhism, quite unacceptable. Be a leader who will fight at a crucial moment to protect the spirit of true Buddhism for posterity.

What does a "crucial moment" mean? The Sokagakkai is a world based on faith, so a crucial moment means general meetings, leaders' meetings and other important activities where your attendance is necessary. The disciples of first President Makiguchi have become top leaders because they supported all important activities for the sake of Kosen-rufu. From the time President Toda was released from prison, they rallied behind him for the progress of the Sokagakkai. Their actions mirror their faith and dedication.

Many of President Toda's youth division members have emerged as today's top leaders. No matter what the occasion, they participated at important meetings without fail, taking responsibility for vital affairs of the Sokagakkai. This also exemplifies unswerving faith.

The person who will proudly achieve victory is the one who takes full responsibility, whether others are watching or not. Avoiding problems is cowardly. If you are inclined to run away from difficulty, you'd better change your attitude. Be a leader who will take the initiative at a crucial moment to protect and advance the organization. If you keep this determination, it will clearly show in every action you take.

The development of leaders

The development of leaders means the development of the Sokagakkai. The progress of leaders toward happiness and human revolution parallels the advance and growth of the organization.

Leaders in our organization are not paid, yet they take care of their members every day. Certainly, it is not easy. But Kosen-rufu means progress, based on our determination to enable all mankind to be happy, in accordance with the will of Nichiren Daishonin. As the President, I cannot do everything by myself, nor do I wish to advance without all of you. You should have confidence in yourselves and guide your members with conviction.

In our organization, you needn't feel hesitant or overly concerned about what others think. Uphold the Gakkai spirit till the end. All leaders should unite and advance toward Kosen-rufu with the same sense of responsibility as the President.

If a leader causes an accident, becomes ill or loses his confidence, many of his members will stop growing in their practice. When a leader practices in high spirits, his members can advance with confidence and courage. Leaders must never be concerned solely with themselves. Never forget, even for a moment, that you are caring for the valuable lives of many Bodhisattvas of the Earth. With this *Ichinen,* a leader will accumulate great fortune.

There are no useless activities in the Sokagakkai. The greater a leader's responsibility, the greater his benefits and the stronger his confidence in the Gohonzon. Faith is the crucial thing. Chant Daimoku with the determination to enable thousands of people to receive benefit from this practice. In this way, you'll definitely develop both the power of Buddha *(Butsu-riki)* and the power of Law *(Ho-riki).*

Don't practice for yourself alone. Become a capable person who practices to achieve Kosen-rufu for the sake of thousands. Faith and practice directed toward this end will enable you to manifest the power of both Law and Buddha.

The people's mind

A Buddhist principle states, "Although one praises the Lotus Sutra, he destroys its intent." When giving guidance, leaders must be in close tune with the member's feelings. Parroting the President's guidance is no more than capitalizing on his name and usually ends in authoritarianism. Instead, give guidance in a way which is natural to you.

Responsibility

A person with a sense of responsibility never forgets his master's guidance but ponders it seriously. He will treasure even one word of his master's guidance and find a way to put it into practice.

Anyone will practice sincerely while his master is present, but a true disciple, one with a feeling of responsibility, will follow his master's guidance even when apart from him.

In the world of Buddhism, self-centered actions destroy our unity *(Ha-wagoso)*. The key to unity is the desire to strive for Buddhism, for the people and for the community. Without a strong sense of responsibility or love for the people, one cannot be called a Gakkai leader.

The brave and the timid

A brave man can surmount any obstacle, but a timid man cannot. Yet, with the guidance and encouragement of their leaders, even the weak can find the strength to break through problems. Timid people, given the right encouragement, can practice as dynamically as the brave.

Deep-rooted faith

For a sapling to grow into a large tree, it must be firmly rooted in the ground. The same principle applies to faith. Being "firmly rooted in faith" means practicing according to the teachings of Nichiren Daishonin, following the organization and maintaining staunch unity. A solitary practice is far from the ideal of deep-rooted faith.

Seniors and juniors

Sakyamuni felt great joy at watching Sharihotsu and his other disciples grow, and he paid them heartfelt respect for their efforts. Sakyamuni totally devoted himself to training disciples for the eternal prosperity of Buddhism.

In the Sokagakkai too, there are many top-level leaders who trust each other and carry out activities in strong unity. Seniors should respect their members and sincerely want them to grow. Juniors should not only respect their seniors but resolve to develop and surpass them, becoming the foundation of the Sokagakkai. Both seniors and juniors alike should hold fast to the Gakkai spirit to ensure the prosperity of Buddhism for the future.

The person who has a firm connection with good leaders will be strong. Strangely, those who remain alone don't develop. Approach your seniors with a seeking spirit and don't rely on cheap tactics. Nothing is stronger than truth, and in the Gakkai, you needn't worry about trying to impress people. What counts is to follow your seniors.

Starting with nothing

Sakyamuni Buddha was born in a palace, but he sought Buddhism and later abandoned his comfortable life in order to attain *enlightenment*. He set out with literally nothing to his name.

Nichiren Daishonin was born to a family of Sudra.[1] He had neither status nor riches. At that time, a heretical priest named Ryokan of Gokurakuji Temple was in league with the ruling Shogunate and acted as if he were enlightened. Ryokan is like many people today who are looked up to as distinguished individuals.

However noble a person may appear, remember that appearances and actual *enlightenment* are two different matters. Buddhism places the greatest value in the plain, unaffected humanity of the common people. In faith, it's okay to start with nothing.

You are a Bodhisattva of the Earth who appeared to show proof of your human revolution through the benefits you receive. Because you have neither riches nor honors nor fame, you are able to prove the benefits of faith exactly as taught in the sutras.

---

[1] Sudra—lowest position in old Indian caste system. Unlike Sakyamuni, the Daishonin appeared as a fisherman's son to prove that even ordinary people can attain *enlightenment*.

Positive and negative

Leaders should have at least one of four characteristics — cheerfulness, a sense of humor, honesty or earnestness. It is ideal if they have all four.

It's better if leaders are positive rather than negative in their outlook. A gloomy, solitary person can't lead many people. Regardless of your problems, you as a leader should always be bright and happy, or your members won't follow you.

Youth

A famous statesman once said, "He who wishes to conquer the world must first of all conquer the sorrow in himself." Battling furiously throughout life against the devil within is Buddhism.

According to a German proverb, nothing is more awesome than still water or a dog that does not bark. Youth should have dignity, like a calm, unfathomable sea. Don't bark like a stray dog over trifles. You should be a self-possessed individual, yet one who, when roused, can display capabilities beyond imagination.

Await the times

An ancient Japanese proverb states, "A fool climbs a tree to see the sunrise, while the wise man waits patiently." However, we must forge ahead, impervious to all obstacles, toward our goal of Kosen-rufu. It may take twenty years to lay a foundation, but the "sun" is already in the sky. We need only wait for the clouds hiding it to clear. To "await the times" means to progress cheerfully with perseverance. It does not mean to be passive and do nothing.

The function of Ichinen

Don't give short-term guidance that applies only to the matter at hand. Your encouragement should live in your members' hearts for a long time. When you base your guidance on Gakkai spirit, they will really grow. Guidance aimed at pure self-advertisement will inevitably bring you to a standstill.

Former President Toda encouraged others with such deep mercy that he'd even tell us, "We'll die together." Nothing is more powerful than mercy. Passion and courage are also vital. So long as you're sincerely thinking of your members' welfare, they will love you, however strict your guidance may be. Even the same words will produce a totally different effect, according to the mysterious function of your *Ichinen*.

Practice first

In any activity, leaders should always put practice first. If, for example, you make everyone else sing Gakkai songs at discussion meetings when you yourself can't lead them properly, it shows you're not taking the meetings seriously. The Sokagakkai does not move by orders. A leader with this careless attitude is sitting on top of the organization.

Have the determination that "I should be the first to know everything." This is the true Gakkai spirit.

Prime motivation

Whether newspapers or magazines praise us or criticize us, remember that it's just a passing phenomenon, much like one cold you catch in the course of your lifetime. Whatever may happen, leaders should not be swayed. Always remember your prime motivation.

Every guidance you receive is like your own reflection. Don't play games or try to go the easy way. An honest approach to faith is the cause for winning in life.

"Eight winds"

Advance confidently and don't be concerned about fame, rumors or criticism. Never play games or use underhanded tactics. Your determined attitude will block the force of the "eight winds" mentioned in the *Gosho:* profit, decline, failure, fame, praise, censure, suffering and pleasure — all of which can weaken a person's faith.

When we truly care about someone, we can tell him the truth, even if it makes him feel resentful. *Zuijii* is the way of the Sokagakkai.

We will carry out Shakubuku, struggling toward Kosen-rufu, till the end of our lives.

Never disgrace Buddhism

There is a saying in the *Gosho, The Law is respected according to the person.* This means that the conduct of leaders can either enhance or disgrace true Buddhism.

Life is but a dream and no one knows for certain whether he will be alive tomorrow. Even though you may become a beggar, do not disgrace the Lotus Sutra. In modern terms, this quotation from the *Gosho* means that, no matter what sort of criticism he may face, one should never disgrace the Sokagakkai.

Sickness and health

In curing sickness, the most important thing is your *Ichinen* to regain your health. If you have this determination, hospital treatment and medication will be more effective than they normally would be. The amazing function of your *Ichinen* is what makes medicine effective. This, in turn, results from a strong practice.

Some illnesses may linger on a great while, but there are none that cannot be cured through sincere chanting to the Gohonzon. When your faith is firmly established, there is no difference between health and sickness. Both are natural conditions, and the potential for both is eternally inherent in our lives.

Faith and physical constitution

Progress in faith changes a person's appearance for the better and strengthens his physical constitution. A sickly appearance may show a lack of good fortune, but it may also indicate that a person is on the verge of changing his destiny.

Never judge the strength of someone's faith from his physical appearance. It's true, however, that one's practice will eventually change his appearance into an energetic and wholesome one.

"Everything's fine"

Time passes relentlessly, and every moment is a struggle. One can never say, "Now, everything's fine." People complain of problems in their districts or chapters, but that's exactly why they are there to guide the members and create unity. In fact, this is the only way that they themselves can grow. If you give up, it's self-defeat.

Chant Daimoku till the last moment of your life and continually renew your determination. This is faith, the spirit of *Hon'in-myo* and the road to *enlightenment.* You should be able to say confidently, at the moment of your death, "Now everything's fine." When Kosen-rufu is achieved, we'll all be able to say, "Everything's fine."

Deep in your heart

Nothing is more important than the *Ichinen* deep in our hearts. When you chant to the Gohonzon and take leadership with the determination to make your members happy, your *Ichinen* will naturally touch their lives.

On the contrary, if you try to order members around with no consideration for them, or if you're thinking of your own glory, you cannot move them, no matter how beautiful your guidance. Authoritarianism is not the Gakkai spirit, nor is it correct faith. No matter how weak a district may be, once you are put in charge, you should make the members feel reassured and confident in their practice. Everything reflects your own *Ichinen*.

When a company president works diligently, so will his employees. But if he doesn't take his job seriously, the employees will be lax and stale, and the working atmosphere will be disrupted. What counts is the leader's *Ichinen*. This applies in both districts and chapters too. Once you practice Buddhism, you will never see a case where a Buddhist principle fails to hold true.

Absolute conviction

In all the universe, I alone am worthy of respect. This means that those who embrace the Gohonzon can manifest the life of *Jo Raku Ga Jo* and achieve absolute happiness. Now in Mappo, only the Daishonin is *worthy of respect*. This statement should be understood from an absolute viewpoint, not a relative one. Since we are all Nichiren Daishonin's disciples, we should be confident that we can attain absolute happiness.

Land borders the sea. Waves ceaselessly dash against the shores, but the land stands firm. Our faith, too, should stand firm against any criticism.

Faith should never become mere habit. We must always advance.

You can enjoy a cool wind while out for a drive, but when the car stops, so does the breeze. Likewise, if you don't progress in faith, happiness cannot come to you.

Human revolution

People won't follow an impatient individual who takes out his frustration on his family when his work doesn't go the way he wants it to. When his attitude improves, so will his work. He can build a harmonious family, carry out his human revolution, and others will then follow him naturally. People follow an individual, not the organization.

⁂

Your surroundings at home or at work may be far from ideal, but whether the atmosphere is bright or dark depends totally on your own *Ichinen*. So long as you blame your situation on external factors, you will never find happiness.

⁂

The *Gosho* states, *If you make infinite effort, even for a single moment, the enlightenment of the True Buddha will be revealed in your life at every moment. Nam-myoho-renge-kyo is an assiduous practice.* When you strengthen your vitality and open up your life by setting a higher goal, everything around you will change. Even if there's a gulf between you and others, it will be resolved quite naturally as you become more broad-minded and understanding.

⁂

For example, an invalid might think, "My life's already over. There's no hope." But when he chants Daimoku, does Shakubuku and decides, "I'm going to live energetically to make others happy," he has started his human revolution. When one acts on his determination to become a leader who can lead hundreds of people to *enlightenment* and absolute happiness, he, too, is achieving his human revolution.

Time

Time is a vital factor in any undertaking. There is a right season, for example, to eat certain fruits such as strawberries, peaches and watermelon. Likewise, never lose a chance to develop yourself. Because you are now followers of the supreme Law, now is the best opportunity to grow.

I dedicated myself to rebuilding the Sokagakkai under the late President, Josei Toda. The benefits which I enjoy today are the fruit of those efforts.

The greatest happiness is being in the Gakkai. If you don't believe it, try doing just as you please for a while without going to any discussion meetings. In very short order, you'll discover that nothing is more enjoyable—or provides greater opportunity for growth—than Gakkai activities.

Mission

Mission is born from self-awakening. Those who live and work amid the realities of daily life and who can realize their mission within its realm are happy. As human beings, these individuals have the loftiest view of life.

A factory worker who resolves to acquire the best skills on the job and pass on his knowledge to many co-workers, is a man with a great mission. Mission does not necessarily mean becoming a high government official or a leading figure. Today's so-called elite are only interested in their own profit and have no elevated sense of mission.

Upholding the mission to help others achieve a fundamental happiness based on the Gohonzon is the noblest way of life.

Patriots

A patriot is a true leader who struggles for the happiness of each individual in the community. For lack of a better standard, society judges people according to their academic history. In the Sokagakkai, however, we consider one's true capability, not his educational background.

General Ney, one of Napoleon's aides, was the son of a blacksmith. I am President of our organization, but I never graduated from college. This shows the spirit of the Sokagakkai. One need not be ashamed merely because he has no college education. Yet we never deny the importance of universities or of the student division. Students should study hard, develop themselves and master their capabilities. Don't forget, though, that faith comes first. Those who have pure, strong faith and who develop their capabilities will enjoy good fortune. This is the law of Buddhism.

Courage

Recently it's become fashionable to talk about having guts. Actually, the greatest courage means unyielding faith, because faith encompasses conviction, continual effort and the power of practice. When one chants Daimoku, he discovers the courage to live strongly with integrity.

Everyone has his own innate character and personality. Some people are warm-hearted, while others are strong-willed. This is a matter of destiny. However, since cause and effect are simultaneous *(Inga Guji)*, once a person embraces the supreme

Law, his life is directed toward happiness. He can break through the limitations of his karma and bring out his full potential. This is why the Gohonzon is absolutely necessary.

During a meeting of the Suikokai[1] I once asked President Toda about the war between the Genji and Heike clans.[2] I said, "Facing swords and arrows must have been terrifying." He answered, "If a man truly understands life, he naturally feels fear." It is human to be afraid and inhuman not to be. It is also natural to feel that war is evil. No one is stronger than the person who has the guts to struggle against war.

A man who knows what to fear and what not to fear and who has conviction is strong. Embracing the Gohonzon requires the greatest courage, which is why our organization is truly strong.

---

[1] Suikokai—group organized by President Toda to train young men as leaders for the future. At Suikokai meetings, he would explain various points of faith using classic novels and biographies as texts. The group was named after the Chinese classic *Suikoden,* the first book used for study.

[2] Genji and Heike—the two most powerful clans in 12th-century Japan. The Heike, who ruled the country, indulged in pleasure-seeking and ignored the plight of the masses, and eventually were overthrown by the Genji.

A true hero

A saying goes, "He who is strong when he stands alone is a true hero." A true hero is one who lives with the Gakkai spirit.

On the contrary, those who pursue social fads, or forget their faith and the Gakkai spirit, or chase after wealth and fame, or act out of habit, are weak even though they may seem strong outwardly. He who upholds the Gakkai spirit until the last moment of his life will be praised by Nichiren Daishonin. He is a true hero, one who stands alone.

From now on, our activities will definitely be carried out on a broader basis. We are entering a time when everything depends on the self-awakening and wisdom of each individual. A man who holds a high objective and shoulders full responsibility will be protected and praised by all Buddhas and Bodhisattvas in the universe.

An old proverb states, "At times an arrow can pierce a rock." A powerful *Ichinen* is the driving force to achieve anything. If even one or two youths are passionately motivated, their spirit will spread like wildfire. Without this spirit, even the best thought-out strategy will fail. The passion and strength of youth are the driving force of everything.

According to circumstances

In the sutras, there is a reference to "thirty-three bodies" and "thirty-four bodies." This means that we must assume many different roles in our activities for Kosen-rufu. Enabling members to progress step by step toward *enlightenment* requires a leader to be strict at times, or even scold them. However, the fundamental *Ichinen* underlying these different roles and activities never changes *(Ichinen Jakusho)*. In the course of our daily lives, that fundamental *Ichinen* is expressed in varying forms to meet the circumstances *(Zuien Shinnyo-no Chi)*.

When you embrace the Gohonzon, you can always act appropriately, according to the situation. The action of *Zuien Shinnyo-no Chi* means doing your best in everything with the awareness that each task or activity is Buddhism itself.

"Always in mind"

When you consistently direct your *Ichinen* toward the Gohonzon, your outlook will change drastically. That's faith. Be strict with yourself to prevent your faith from becoming mere habit. Encouraging each other is also fundamental to our organization and creates harmonious unity *(Wagoso)* among all the members.

A Buddha is one who works incessantly to help others attain *enlightenment.* Gakkai leaders should constantly be thinking of their members' happiness. This is what Buddhism terms *Maiji sa ze nen.* It also applies to a scholar who goes to sleep and wakes up still thinking of his research. Attaining happiness, however, requires *Maiji sa ze nen* in faith.

Impartiality

The President is the center of the Sokagakkai, and therefore, he cannot be partial. Merely because he is friendly with someone, he must not show favoritism to him in public affairs. If he did, those who are practicing earnestly might stop trying. Were he to give special consideration to his relatives, the organization would come to ruin.

For example, even if a top senior who is personally honored and respected should prove to be incapable, he should not hold an important position. If leaders are swayed by emotion, the whole organization will collapse and members will lose their passion to practice. Still, you should have the determination to be someone who is deeply considerate.

Those who are sincerely fighting for Kosenrufu should all be treasured. In faith and activities, you should never label people or try to categorize them.

Time will tell a man's value

Sometimes things go smoothly and sometimes they don't. You cannot measure a man's true greatness just by one or two years of success. Often it takes ten or even twenty years before his true value becomes apparent.

I never judge a man by his past actions. Since cause and effect are simultaneous, the reality of the present moment is what counts. My fervent desire is to make everyone develop and become happy, without a single exception, regardless of his past successes or failures.

Formality

At meetings, it is vital to create a relaxed atmosphere where people can listen comfortably. The important thing is progress in their faith.

It is wrong and undemocratic to insist on formality or a militaristic manner. Gakkai members include students, factory workers, businessmen, housewives and professionals, and a leader must help all of them understand this practice. Whether giving guidance or leading meetings, he must create an atmosphere of strong faith, which includes everyone, just as a broad river enfolds everything in its course. Avoid empty formality at all cost.

Rumors

Nothing is more unreliable than a rumor. When you hear rumors about yourself—whether flattering or critical—you'll lose out if you're influenced by them. Anyone who gets swell-headed and thinks he's great when someone praises him, is shallow and has weak faith.

With a proper yardstick, you can listen to any story and know if the person telling it is trying to get attention, lying, defending himself, exaggerating or playing games. If you use sincere faith in the Gohonzon as your standard, you won't be influenced and you can judge correctly.

The age of Honmon

The age of *Honmon* is the time when actual proof of the Daishonin's Buddhism, appearing in the form of gain or loss, will become much clearer. Those who act against true Buddhism will suffer loss, while those who practice sincerely gain immense fortune.

Former President Toda often said, "The sun is now high overhead." Be utterly confident that now, right now, is the time when actual proof of the Gohonzon will become obvious and practice for all you're worth.

Chapter Three: Unity

Decision-making

Some 800 years ago, Minamoto Yoritomo,[1] commander of the Genji clan, lost the battle of Ishibashiyama and fled to the Boso district (presently Chiba Prefecture). He asked Kazusa-Gonnosuke Hirotsune, the head of a powerful clan in that area, to raise an army with him against the ruling Heike clan. However, Hirotsune pondered for three days and nights before deciding. When he finally agreed, Yoritomo refused his aid, saying, "You're too late. Your resolution fails to impress me."

The authenticity of these words has never been proven, and the quote may have been fictionalized by a historian. At any rate, Hirotsune felt at a loss, unsure of whether Yoritomo — who did not even have an army — could win or not.

Decision-making is the most important thing you have to do in life.

---

[1] Minamoto Yoritomo (1147-99)—founded the Kamakura regime. Two rival clans dominated 12th-century Japan: the Genji and the decadent Heike, who ruled the country. As leader of the Genji clan, Yoritomo was viewed as a definite threat by the Heike, who exiled him to Izu Peninsula. Nevertheless, he plotted and raised an army. His forces were defeated at Ishibashiyama, but he escaped and again rallied support. Eventually he defeated the Heike in a spectacular sea battle at Dan-no Ura and established a military government in Kamakura.

Win or lose

You will lose the battle if you're unassertive or swayed by sympathy or a debt of gratitude or if you forget the larger scope of things. Leaders must lead with a dauntless attitude.

Tokugawa Ieyasu,[1] the founder of the Edo government, won his first battle when he was only eighteen. Sometime later, the powerful general, Imagawa Yoshimoto, advanced on Kyoto, the capital, with Ieyasu's forces supporting his own. When Yoshimoto was defeated by Oda Nobunaga at Okehazama, Ieyasu and his troops pulled out and retreated, without losing a single man.

The priest Sessai, who educated Ieyasu from childhood, taught him, "Never lose in battle. Otherwise, the entire clan will be ruined. Win, whatever it takes." Sessai is said to have drilled Ieyasu thoroughly on this point.

---

[1] Tokugawa Ieyasu (1542-1616)—founder of the Edo government. As a boy, he was taken hostage by the powerful warlord Imagawa Yoshimoto. His men were also obliged to become Yoshimoto's vassals. Years later, when Yoshimoto was defeated at Okehazama by Oda Nobunaga, Ieyasu seized the opportunity and fled with his men to freedom. He later supported Nobunaga, and in return, the old Tokugawa estates were restored to him. After the death of Nobunaga's successor, Toyotomi Hideyoshi, Ieyasu defeated the Toyotomi forces at Sekigahara. In 1603 he established the Edo government which lasted 262 years.

Buddhism is win or lose. We must never forget that spirit, even for a moment.

Weakness

Among the many warlords of feudal Japan, Tokugawa Ieyasu was second to none in his concern for his men. Toyotomi Hideyoshi[1] failed because he was too indulgent toward his soldiers.

It might seem kinder to let leaders do as they please, but sometimes it's an act of mercy *(Jihi)* to scold or encourage them on the basis of faith itself.

It is said that at nineteen, Ieyasu realized, "People will not be led by humane consideration alone. Such feelings are my weakness. If I let it show, it will cause trouble among my soldiers." I think Ieyasu's idea is not right in all respects, but there is some truth in it. One must not reveal his weakness when in battle.

---

[1] Toyotomi Hideyoshi (1536-98)—great warlord of feudal era. Born a low-ranking foot-soldier, he longed to become a great samurai. His gift for strategy impressed Oda Nobunaga, who employed him. Hideyoshi conquered many warlords, and when Nobunaga was killed, he succeeded him. His clan was defeated by the Tokugawas after his death.

In our case, when our faith becomes weak, the members won't follow us. If you try to solve a problem by methods and tactics alone, it will definitely create conflict. Nowadays many people think that showing one's weakness is a sign of humanity. Concerning faith, however, always be resolute. So long as your faith is firm, conflicts will disappear.

Bad luck

A question was put to a certain warlord who surrendered and was taken into the presence of Toyotomi Hideyoshi. "Are you a lucky or unlucky man?" The lord replied, "I am unlucky," upon which Hideyoshi refused to use him saying, "I cannot take an unlucky man on my side." Later, the unfortunate lord joined forces with Ishida Mitsunari and was killed in the defeat at Sekigahara.[1]

In light of the Buddhist principle of *Esho Funi,* a general will lose his own fortune if he is surrounded by unlucky or evil men.

---

[1] Sekigahara—after Toyotomi Hideyoshi's death, Ishida Mitsunari rallied other warlords in an attempt to restore the Toyotomi clan's prestige. They confronted Tokugawa Ieyasu in a struggle for virtual control of Japan and were defeated at the battle of Sekigahara in 1600.

Oda Nobunaga had a harsh nature like autumn frost or the scorching sun. Hideyoshi, however, was wise enough to be cheerful. When he entered a gloomy room, it would light up as though the sun had risen. You should take cheerfulness into consideration, too.

Humanism

Of the three warlords, Nobunaga, Hideyoshi and Ieyasu, Hideyoshi can be considered the most humane. We, ourselves, are training new leaders for the age to come, in accordance with the Buddhist principle: "Because the Law is supreme, the man who embraces it is also noble." Such leaders will possess the merits of these three generals, as well as their own unique talents. However, there is no need to imitate particlular aspects of some hero's personality. One should develop his own character.

The Daishonin's Buddhism is the only true standard by which to judge a person's greatness. Whether one becomes famous or not depends on mere chance. One should become a leader with a humanistic philosophy.

Philosophy for living

Hideyoshi was also heroic in that he formulated his own philosophy through action. He desired fame and a successful career and shaped his life to achieve it. Both his philosophy and way of life were geared toward realizing his own objectives. With the Daishonin's life-philosophy as the basis, you can gauge the real merits of heroes.

Realizing our own happiness and enabling others to become happy — this ideal and its application constitute our philosophy. That's why there is a great difference between Hideyoshi's philosophy and our own, both in scope and in depth. Those who embrace the supreme Law are the true heroes and leaders of a new age.

Live with the people

Lenin is said to have voluntarily shared the life of common laborers. He can be called great in that respect. In appearing no different from an ordinary person, he displayed the Buddhist principle of *Jido Bompu*. So long as leaders act in this way, democracy can endure. Otherwise, it will degenerate into bureaucracy and authoritarianism.

We must eternally advance with the people.

Behind the scenes

Kei Hara,[1] an active politician at the turn of the century, was great because of his unseen yet painstaking efforts to weigh and direct the course of the nation.

For the sake of the future, Sokagakkai leaders must seriously consider and take responsibility for things that other people don't think about. Kosen-rufu cannot be achieved without those who struggle behind the scenes.

Harmony

Takamori Saigo[2] said, "Reward a person for his services. At times it is necessary to boldly promote a younger man, always considering how to put the right person in the right place."

A leader should know how to employ his men to the best advantage and assess the current of the times. He should always view things from an overall perspective. Never make short-sighted moves based solely on your personal feelings.

---

[1] Kei Hara (1856-1921)—established party politics in Japan. He was famed as a spokesman of the common man.

[2] Takamori Saigo (1827-1877)—gifted leader of Meiji Restoration. Helped negotiate surrender of Tokugawas in 1868.

The contrabass lends depth and harmony to an orchestra's overall sound. This is like the role of a conservative, senior citizen.

In our organization, it's ideal when the young members have high spirits while older members have dignity and serve as a firm foundation.

Hero of the press

Unless backed by a sound philosophy, any effort you undertake will eventually collapse. Viscount Northcliffe, the British newspaper king, was fascinated by the printing press from the age of eight. He later became a heroic publisher who, behind the scenes, exerted great influence on the English political world.

Northcliffe was called the Napoleon of England. He determined that in whatever action he took, despite any hardships, there could be no compromise. He carried out his original intention regardless of the difficulties he encountered.

Great are those individuals who fulfill their beliefs throughout their lifetimes, even though they may not be significant nor deal with faith. Those who backslide or lose heart halfway are cowards.

Human greatness

In the novel, *The Eternal City,* Rossi is a youthful revolutionary and Bruno, his devoted comrade. Even while being tortured by his prosecutors and forced to listen to their malign criticism of Rossi, Bruno never gave up his trust in his friend. He chose death, crying out, "Long live Rossi!" It is true that Bruno's life was not as colorful as Rossi's, but in comparing the two, I think that Bruno was the greater man.

Carelessness

Napoleon was exiled to Elba Island after his first defeat, but he escaped and recruited 200,000 soldiers in just three months. Tens or hundreds of thousands of people will sympathize with the ideal of a single person if his heart is burning with a sense of purpose. This exemplifies a leader's *Ichinen.*

Napoleon was defeated at Waterloo in June, 1815, by the allied forces of England and Prussia under the command of Wellington and Blücher. As one story goes, the outcome of the battle was determined by three persons — Napoleon,

Wellington and a farmer who showed one of Napoleon's generals the wrong road.

Napoleon's forces were supposedly destroyed through the carelessness of a general named Ney. Defeat became a foregone conclusion when Ney's army was delayed thirty minutes. The battle might have ended in an overwhelming victory for Napoleon, had he arrived on time.

According to the story, Ney stopped enroute to the battle to ask directions from a farmer - actually a spy - and was thoroughly duped. It was no more than a moment's negligence on his part. He had scrupulously executed all of Napoleon's orders, up till the moment when his crack cavalry units found themselves in a swamp. His carelessness in not questioning the farmer's trustworthiness brought about Napoleon's downfall.

This particular case in the history of warfare shows how crucial a leader is. A general is highly respected and trusted by his men, but if he blunders, he betrays them all. Carelessness is one's greatest enemy. The farmer was a Frenchman.

He was so to speak, a parasite in a lion's body. A leader must be able to spot such things.

A leader's spirit

An anecdote has it that during an air raid, while bombs were falling, Sir Winston Churchill strolled down the street tossing a ball. Churchill's unruffled composure reassured his countrymen as though he were saying, "Don't worry, we can't help but win."

This story may or may not be true, but it reflects the kind of undaunted readiness to face the world which top leaders should have.

Disciples

How many Communists today are still struggling for world revolution in the true spirit of Nikolai Lenin? Shoin Yoshida[1] and Yukichi Fukuzawa[2] were also great pioneers. Yet, how many of their

---

[1]Shoin Yoshida (1830-1859)—Confucian scholar, twice imprisoned for efforts at progressive social reform. Many of his followers later became leaders of Meiji Restoration. Executed at age twenty-nine.

[2]Yukichi Fukuzawa (1835-1901)—great thinker and educator who contributed to modernization of Japan. Outstanding works include *An Exhortation Toward Learning* and *An Outline of the Theory of Civilization*.

disciples still uphold their ideals and fight for them in society? How many, in their lifetimes, have proven the greatness of their teachers?

Among the followers of great thinkers, statesmen, economists or scientists, very few could rightly be called true disciples. Almost none have struggled to carry on their teachers' work in the spirit of creating the greatest good for humanity.

We are the eternal disciples and children of Nichiren Daishonin. The young people who gathered under former President Toda are still fighting to carry out his goal. Their conduct is unprecedented in history and proves the greatness of their master.

Learning

Yukichi Fukuzawa was a pioneer of education in the Meiji era. During the fierce battle between the Imperial forces and Shogi-tai[1] en-

---

[1] Shogi-tai—when Emperor Meiji was restored to the throne in 1868, the old Tokugawa government agreed to surrender Edo Castle. However, the Tokugawa warriors rebelled, forming a company called the Shogi-tai to resist the Imperial forces, but were totally defeated.

trenched in the forests of Ueno, Fukuzawa calmly continued lecturing on economics at his private school in Tokyo, even amid the roar of the cannon.

Fukuzawa said, "Those who never stop learning are truly brave." We who study and practice the supreme Law in this corrupt and gaudy age can be called true pioneers and men of courage.

Cheerful Shakubuku

Shakubuku is the Buddhist practice. Since it is a difficult practice, it may not always be enjoyable. When you encourage your members to do Shakubuku, be like a great teacher who captivates his students and enables them to fully grasp the subject.

A book by Albert Einstein uses interesting descriptions and avoids complicated mathematical formulas in letting the reader understand physics. Former President Toda's lectures were truly enjoyable and encouraged people to carry out their faith. The same idea is true of Shakubuku.

Guidance depends on the person who gives it. Cheerful Shakubuku will result when you warmly guide troubled members so they can have confidence in themselves, change their karma and obtain great benefits. For this reason, you should first of all chant Daimoku and develop yourself by revealing the power of the supreme Law. Your voice will then stir people when you give guidance.

Shakubuku is hard. That's why it is enjoyable and brings great benefits. If a university diploma were easily obtained, what real satisfaction would there be? When our painstaking effort pays off and even one or two people receive the Gohonzon, we are delighted. All the difficulties we encountered up till then are immediately changed to *enlightenment.*

Hunger is the best seasoning, as the saying goes. You cannot enter college without meeting the requirements, and you cannot attain *enlightenment* without practice. This is called *Bonno soku Bodai.* There is no *enlightenment* without desires, and without hardship, there is no happiness.

Courage, capacity and wisdom

Former President Toda sometimes took what seemed too severe an attitude towards the leaders. He was especially strict in training youth. He often used to cite the example of the sea bass in the Sea of Genkai. Buffeted by the unusually rough currents there, they become lean and extra delicious. The same holds true with people. Men should undergo strict training while young.

Takeda Shingen,[1] a general of Japan's civil war era, said, "Men are the moats, the castle walls and the castle itself." The Sokagakkai is a castle of capable people. Three qualities are required of a great individual: courage, capacity and wisdom. Become a person who embodies all three, so you can solve difficult problems calmly, regardless of whether you're praised or censured.

Unity

Our organization will never be destroyed by external forces. The *Sado Gosho* reads, *Non-Buddhists or evil men can never destroy the Buddha's true teachings, but the disciples of the Buddha definitely could. The parasite in a lion's body devours him. . .* Cold wind toughens one's skin, but a diseased organ will kill him. What matters is the internal unity of the organization.

---

[1] Takeda Shingen (1521-73)—famous warlord from the province of Kai (present-day Yamanashi). Tradition has it that unlike other great warlords of the day, he never built a castle, relying instead on the capabilities and unity of his men.

Even a massive tree can rot, as it is helpless against termites. It can endure harsh rain and snow storms, but cannot combat those insects which bore from within. Many people die in traffic accidents, but even more die from internal diseases. Our organization will not be shaken in the least by any clamor from the outside world. Internal unity is crucial.

Teamwork

In the 1964 Olympics, the Japanese women's volleyball team defeated the powerful Russian team. Player for player, the Japanese women were physically weaker than the Russians, and their technique was probably not as polished. But they did have a burning determination to win no matter what, and in addition, they had splendid teamwork. Rigorous training and the power of unity gave victory to the Japanese team.

Ultimately, whether or not one has confidence will decide the outcome of anything. Since we strive with confidence and unity, we can always win. On the stage of the universe, believers in the supreme Law will never be defeated, but will win a succession of victories in their ongoing struggle.

Harmonious unity is the key to victory in any campaign. Victory or defeat hinges on unity. Everything accomplished so far in the Sokagakkai has been the result of unity. If unity is lacking or weak, good results cannot be achieved.

Communication

It is vital that leaders communicate thoroughly about even the smallest details so that they can keep pace with each other. This is similar to a centipede race, in which the runners have their legs tied to one another. If one runner stumbles, the whole team falls. One individual's failure can cause trouble for an entire group.

One must always communicate what he considers important as soon as he hears about it. Otherwise, our organization cannot advance. If all the leaders can keep up with each other, the organization will be that much stronger.

Communication and reports must be clear-cut. Be careful to communicate thoroughly and regard the organization as a living body. This is a cause for further development. Paying constant attention to this point shows the spirit of *Maiji sa ze nen.*

Leaders should be especially responsible about communicating and reporting.

༺༻

Those who neglect communication or reports are, in a sense, evil.

༺༻

A report is the first step toward the next victory. President Toda used to say that the leader who fails to report is an enemy. He may praise true Buddhism, but he isn't really practicing. When a person is determined to communicate and report, his practice is dynamic. In Buddhism, to avoid reporting is irresponsible.

༺༻

Whether at work or in activities, leaders especially should let others know where they will be. This is one aspect of unity. If members cannot find their leader, there is no way they can carry out harmonious activities. The important point is not whether you're here or there, but that you communicate. Good communication is vital in building a harmonious environment.

Solitary Bodhisattvas

In the 15th chapter of the Lotus Sutra, there is a description of countless Bodhisattvas emerging from the earth *(Jiyu-no Bosatsu)*. Among them were "solitary Bodhisattvas" who, as the sutra states, "sought to be alone, were solitary and without fellow Bodhisattvas." Those who strive to maintain solidarity can accumulate good fortune. Self-satisfied people are "solitary Bodhisattvas" and cannot accumulate fortune.

The new leaders of the future should not be hero-types who handle matters merely with their own skills. A good leader is one who can harmonize all the people in a group, be it company or home, so that they can work smoothly, putting their individual potential into full use.

Championship game

In the fall of 1965, Waseda University defeated Keio University in baseball. There were many reasons for this. One was that Waseda, having suffered repeated defeat at the hands of the Keio team, was determined to beat them at all cost. Another factor was Waseda's excellent manager. He always kept a cheerful attitude and inspired his men with unshakable confidence, enabling them to throw themselves totally into their game.

~~~

Report also has it that the Keio team was preparing for a victory parade before the game began. Spoiled by their many victories, they mistakenly focused their efforts on a point other than winning. On the other hand, the Waseda stands were filled long before the start of the game. Victory requires maximum effort. Concentrating on the wrong point was carelessness on Keio's part.

Harmonious unity

We often stress following the organization, but the basis of this is nothing other than the Gohonzon. In the Sokagakkai, the President is the central leader and carries the heaviest responsibility. The supreme Law is fundamental, but it takes a human being to give guidance and enable other people to understand that Law. This is a leader's responsibility.

Each area has a headquarters chief, and members should try to receive as much guidance as they can from him. These actions add up to following the organization. However, the basis of unity must always be the Gohonzon and the practice of *Itai Doshin*. People who remain apart from the organization do not develop.

The Sutra teaches the principle of *Wagoso*, or harmonious unity. In modern terms, this refers to our organization.

Strategy

There is a *Gosho* passage that states, *They plotted their strategy in camp to win a victory a thousand miles away.* This spirit is necessary in making plans and should be part of all our activities. Plans should clearly reflect the opinions of everyone and result in a positive conclusion. Otherwise, obstacles cannot be overcome.

Sacrifice

The Nichirenshoshu Sokagakkai has faced many persecutions in the course of its history. Yet it has become what it is today because of the greatness of the Law, and because its first president, Makiguchi, and second president, Toda, fought without retreating a single step.

Today, the time is ripe for Kosen-rufu. No authority can touch us if we simply maintain our faith and unity.

However, we must not be careless. The most

powerful of devils *(Dairokuten-no Mao)* and the severest of obstacles *(Sanrui-no Goteki)* can appear at any time. Without obstacles and devils, we cannot attain *enlightenment*. We must unite firmly and overcome all obstacles in our progress toward the peace and happiness of people everywhere.

There is no such thing as sacrifice in Buddhism. Individuals like President Makiguchi and the three martyrs of Atsuhara may appear to have sacrificed themselves, but in reality, they acted as they wished to and so attained *enlightenment*. They were not victims in any sense. On the contrary, in all past revolutions, blood has been shed and families destroyed, and the victims — both leaders and the people — have suffered miserably.

Shakubuku spirit

No matter what the age, the Sokagakkai will always be a movement of Shakubuku. Though it has met with every form of opposition and abuse, the Sokagakkai has developed to what it is today by carrying out the Shakubuku spirit. We will maintain this same spirit in the future. The true spirit of Shakubuku is mercy, and the basis of our organization must be nothing but Shakubuku.

⚜

Because the customs and manners of each area are different, unique circumstances will arise. But the fundamental Gakkai spirit should never change. At times, it's a good idea to adapt our practice to a particular area's culture, according to the principle of *Zuiho Bini,* but this is strictly of secondary importance. The basis of *Zuiho Bini* is faith, which can change the environment. The important thing is building an ideal society through the principle of *Esho Funi,* based on individual human revolution.

⚜

Before World War II, when numerous Japanese emigrated to Manchuria, there was a reported increase in thunderstorms, rare until that time. The northern areas of Tohoku and Hokkaido have, with the increase in population, experienced less snow than previously. This is proof that human actions permeate and affect the universe.

Likewise, even the gloomiest, weakest individual can become dynamic when he chants Daimoku courageously. This principle applies equally to a family or to the land they live in. Don't be overly influenced by customs and manners. Our religious revolution will transform them, infusing local traditions with renewed and positive meaning.

The challenge is to win

A famous saying goes, "The best defense is a good offense." To win means to attack; defense alone will never bring victory. Steady progress leads to victory in any campaign.

For example, a salesman can't do business if he waits for his customers to come to him. He can only sell through consistent and direct salesmanship. A detective can arrest a criminal only after making exhaustive efforts to collect sufficient evidence and track down his man.

No one is going to wait for you to Shakubuku him. It takes thousands upon thousands of waves dashing against the rocks at the ocean's edge to wear them down. In the same way, you must chant Daimoku over and over to help even one person attain happiness. Shakubuku is the religious revolution which will bring about Kosen-rufu.

The *Gosho* states, *Nam-myoho-renge-kyo is assiduous practice.* The basis of faith is to chant Daimoku throughout your lifetime. This is the practice of the Buddhist principle: "Faith equals daily life."

Unifying ideologies

In Japan today there are an estimated 180,000 religious groups, including Buddhists and Christians. Japan is truly a mecca of religions. In this sense, there is no country like Japan in the world.

The Soviet Union and mainland China are dominated by communism, while Western nations like the United States are primarily influenced by Christianity. Hinduism, and in some parts, Buddhism, prevail in India. Thailand has Hinayana Buddhism, while Islam is dominant in the Arab nations. Generally speaking, each nation has its own religious belief.

Yet no one knows precisely which specific religion the Japanese believe in. This is proof of the present confusion of thought in Japan. Because their philosophies are confused, the people are confused too, and the nation is disunited.

As the spirit of Shakubuku rises among the people and the supreme Buddhism of *Shiki Shin Funi* forms the pillar of man's philosophy, peace and stability will spread throughout the world. However, unifying ideologies in no way implies the rejection of other philosophies and religions. When viewed in the light of Buddhism, they can serve as a preface to its teachings and be applied constructively.

If the majority of a nation's people practice Nichiren Daishonin's Buddhism, while the rest all understand its teachings, that nation will naturally be protected.

Shakubuku

If Shakubuku were easy, it would not be Shakubuku. You'll experience great joy when you've tried earnestly and finally have convinced another person to practice. It is the true spirit of Buddhism to do your utmost in your own situation.

Things may not always go as you expect, but so long as you keep a sincere *Ichinen,* results will appear at crucial moments. This is inconspicuous benefit *(Myoyaku)* and the law of Buddhism. So long as you have this conviction, you will truly enjoy your life and be protected by the *Shoten Zenjin.*

Few people have found Shakubuku to be as easy as they expected. Yet, so long as you do Shakubuku, you will definitely receive benefits. Show through your actions that Shakubuku is an enjoyable practice and thus inspire other members to do it. You will gain energy through Shakubuku. This is the supreme Law and the guidance of the Sokagakkai.

You do not practice Buddhism for your district chief's sake, nor do you do Shakubuku for your chapter chief. Shakubuku is the teaching of Nichiren Daishonin, and you do it for your own sake. We do Shakubuku because it is the only practice in this age of Mappo. There is no other way to change one's destiny. Shakubuku is solely for the purpose of changing one's karma. The role of the organization lies in enabling members to practice Shakubuku easily.

Shakubuku is an absolutely necessary practice.

The important thing is encouraging people to do it. Don't browbeat your members when they're already trying their best. Show them how to do Shakubuku happily and patiently so they can persevere in their efforts.

Time, place and man

Three conditions needed to achieve anything are opportunity, natural advantage and the unity of men.

Opportunity means that the time has come when Nichiren Daishonin's Buddhism is needed. From a dialectical viewpoint of thesis, antithesis and synthesis, a philosophy must naturally emerge which can guide both materialism and spiritualism. Though contemporary intellectuals may criticize Buddhism, they are totally ignorant of its teachings. It is pointless to listen to other people's opinions about Buddhism. They will never understand, unless we teach them. This is *Zuijii* and the practice of Shakubuku. We should not be swayed by those around us.

Advantages of nature can be understood by

means of reverse example. An isolated building in the middle of the African desert would be useless. A factory in the mountain recesses of Hokkaido would be equally useless because of the difficulty of transporting raw materials and manufactured products. In business or in any other ventures, one of course takes natural advantages into consideration.

If the head temple, Daisekiji, were situated in a cold, desolate area or on top of a mountain, it would be hard for elderly people to travel there. Because Buddhism is for the happiness of the people, the head temple is located where it is.

Relationship to Buddhism

Nothing is stronger than unity among people. Based on the Gohonzon, we unite with the spirit of *Itai Doshin* while respecting each other's strengths and individuality and encouraging one another. This is the Sokagakkai. There are no factions in our organization. The individual who breaks our unity *(Ha-Wagoso)* is evil.

Whether or not a person embraces the Gohonzon depends on his past relationship with Buddhism. You needn't regret that your parents don't practice, so long as you're showing them the benefits of the Gohonzon. Many people have this problem.

Don't be sorry you're the only one practicing in your family. Nichiren Daishonin taught that even one person attaining *enlightenment* will secure the happiness of his entire family. Your efforts now will eventually enable your whole family to chant.

Developing people one by one

From now on, it's important to help each member solidify his faith without waiting for specific instructions to do so. If we develop capable leaders out of those members now practicing, we can achieve Kosen-rufu. Of course, this doesn't mean we no longer have to do Shakubuku. Shakubuku is the source of benefit.

Never be fanatical in doing Shakubuku. Many people now recognize the Sokagakkai, and we can enable them to gain a further understanding through a broadened scope of cultural activities.

Shakubuku, action of the highest good

Those who continue to chant sincere Daimoku

and advance toward their *enlightenment* no matter what, are the treasures of the Sokagakkai.

Carrying out activities for the sake of Kosen-rufu is action of the highest good. Shakubuku is the surest way to great benefits and is far more rewarding than saving thousands of drowning people or receiving the Nobel Prize. This is what Nichiren Daishonin taught.

Faith first

With the principle of "faith first," a leader can give clear-cut guidance. He can also win in his campaigns, and ill-feelings *(Onshitsu)* among his members will disappear. If he forgets this principle, he will naturally complicate matters and stop progressing. Eventually, his confidence will give way.

When you chant Daimoku with another member, you can gauge the condition of his faith. Even if someone believes in "faith first," it may fall into the realm of mere theory. Faith is nothing but practice.

Faith means to practice Buddhism. Therefore, any individual who practices can achieve his human revolution. Many people talk about human revolution in an abstract or theoretical way, but it's meaningless without actual proof of their happiness and change of character. Those who chant lots of Daimoku will have clear, shining complexions and be bright and vigorous. No matter how much work they have, they will not be discouraged in the least. The important thing is daily practice. Practice itself is the study of Buddhism.

Master and disciple

In one sense, the Gohonzon is our master and we, the disciples. Buddhism teaches the inseparability of master and disciple, or *Shitei Funi.* "Inseparable" means never to doubt or forsake the Gohonzon no matter what happens. It is not *Shitei Funi* when one decides to stop practicing because a leader corrects him or because something goes wrong. One who practices to the Gohonzon throughout his lifetime exemplifies *Shitei Funi.*

Through striving to realize *Shitei Funi,* we begin to fuse our lives with that of the Gohonzon. This is called *Kyochi Myogo* and enables us to attain *enlightenment.* The Sokagakkai is a lay organization devoted to Shakubuku. When we stand up as Sokagakkai members and strive for Kosen-rufu, our faith establishes the true bond of master and disciple between ourselves and Nichiren Daishonin.

Leaders are all fellow disciples and should respect one another. A chapter chief and his members do not have a master-disciple relationship. They strive together as fellow disciples, and their relationship is one of good friends *(Zenchishiki),* not master and disciples. Never make the bad cause of distorting the master-disciple relationship.

One should not keep his master's guidance only to himself. He is not a disciple unless he can correctly relay the guidance to his fellow members and elaborate on it. The master gives guidance to all members through one person. *Shitei Funi* is realized only when a disciple puts his master's guidance into practice.

Nichiren Daishonin and Nikko Shonin together inscribed Gohonzons and wrote several letters. A Sokagakkai leader without a strong connection to his master is not living up to the principle of *Shitei Funi.*

Daily practice

Everyone is busy and preoccupied with his own worries. What Buddhism terms *Shaba,* or this world, is another word for endurance. Even children are busy playing. Baseball players, their fans and television personalities are all caught up in their responsibilities. Even sick people are occupied in a way. Because we are busy, yet still carry out our practice, we are assured of great benefits.

A *Gosho* passage states, *One day's practice in the mundane world is far more valuable than a hundred years' practice in paradise.* If a hundred years' effort were not enough to make the cause for *enlightenment,* life would be meaningless. When one practices the supreme Law of Buddhism, even for a single day, he can accumulate both fortune and wisdom, making life truly purposeful.

A golden age

Kosen-rufu can be compared to a golden age in which people will develop "golden" lives, both materially and spiritually. In the *Ongi Kuden,* the four sufferings of birth, old age, sickness and death *(Sho Ryo Byo Shi)* are compared to the four elements of gold, silver, copper and iron. Gold is likened to life. To be alive is golden.

Gold is invaluable and has numerous uses. In this sense, gold is a "living" metal. For us, gold refers to the principle that faith equals daily life, which enables us to enjoy life to the fullest.

The purest organization

Members should not loan money to one another nor, as a general rule, go into business together. The basic principle of the Sokagakkai is that members protect the Gohonzon by carrying out their faith and strive for the sake of Kosen-rufu. Taking advantage of faith for selfish purposes is an evil action.

Therefore, until Kosen-rufu is achieved, leaders must take the initiative, unite and strive for the happiness of the people by protecting the Sokagakkai. Sokagakkai members are all people of integrity. We must not let even the slightest corruption enter our organization.

"Return to the Daishonin's age"

"Return to the Daishonin's age" means that we should carry out our faith as direct disciples of Nichiren Daishonin. Although exiled twice, to Sado Island and to the Izu Peninsula, the Daishonin devoted his entire life to activities for Kosen-rufu. The Sokagakkai carries out its actions in exactly the same spirit.

We now have many splendid community centers. As conditions for Kosen-rufu improve, it will be all too easy for people to become entrenched in formalities and lose the original faith which the Daishonin exemplified. This is why second President Toda re-affirmed the spirit of "returning to the Daishonin's age."

Our faith, above all, should mean what it did in the days of Nichiren Daishonin. Any organization or religious group tends to lose its fundamental spirit as time passes. After thirty or forty years, Sokagakkai members will all have established their own places in society and achieved happiness. Scores of community centers will have been completed. At that time, we should repeatedly proclaim, "Return to the early days of the Sokagakkai!" Leaders must never forget the spirit with which our organization was founded, and they should pass this spirit on to their members. They should develop the kind of faith that Nichiren Daishonin would praise and take pride in their struggle.

"Indestructible as a diamond"

Buddhism explains the principle: "indestructible as a diamond." This means that through faith, we establish a life-condition as eternally bright and lasting as a precious gem.

The life of Nichiren Daishonin is the prime example. As we worship the Gohonzon, the same *enlightenment* wells up from our lives, too, enabling us to attain the same supreme life-condition.

"Indestructible as a diamond" means that we can gain fortune and be absolutely confident throughout the long voyage of life.

Building this fortune and confidence and achieving your human revolution depend solely upon faith. The human mind changes moment by moment. No one has control over this. Through powerful faith and sincere Daimoku, however, you can naturally overcome this inborn characteristic and attain Buddhahood.

People who stubbornly cling to one-sided opinions or who criticize will suffer and make those around them miserable too. Maintain pure faith and chant Daimoku powerfully, like raging waves. Those individuals who have resolved to chant Daimoku throughout their lifetimes and to commit their lives to the goal of the Sokagakkai will achieve *enlightenment* as indestructible as a diamond.

The greatness of the Gohonzon

Former President Toda once said, "The Gohonzon is indeed great, but since our practice seems so simple, people can't believe it works." For example, when the telephone was invented, people were astonished that it was so easy and convenient. Today, however, we take the telephone and other modern conveniences for granted.

Out of four billion people in the world today, only 20 million know the power of the Gohonzon. The others are quite unaware of it. People didn't trust the telephone when it first appeared. Of course the Gohonzon is based on the principle which clarifies the nature of life and is infinitely more profound than the telephone. Perhaps people mistrust it just because of its simplicity, which is a very human reaction. As science develops, philosophy advances and the validity of Buddhism becomes more evident, they will understand it readily.

In the present age of Mappo, the greatest benefits come from creating harmonious unity *(Wagoso)*. In the Zoho period, benefits came from building temples. Today, this means building an organization to achieve Kosen-rufu, which will bring far greater benefits than erecting temples in Zoho.

Buddhism is win or lose

People who have the courage to seek and learn for themselves are truly great. One's faith can only be judged from a lifelong perspective. Buddhism is eternal and spells either victory or defeat. No matter how hard you plot and scheme, without faith, you will eventually lose and be unhappy. The individual who practices sincerely will ultimately win and enjoy good fortune. This is the way of Buddhism.

Winning or losing in Buddhism is another name for the eternal struggle with devils *(Ma)*. Whether you win or lose depends entirely on the strength of your faith. Never complain, but face the Gohonzon with an undaunted attitude.

Great fortune

The late President Toda would often say, "It is due to my struggle against oppression by the militarist regime that I enjoy immense benefits today. I have been able to establish this great fortune because I was imprisoned two years for the sake of the Gohonzon."

I, too, enjoy great happiness now because I followed President Toda to the end and fought bravely together with him when he was facing his greatest hardships.

More complex than a TV

No matter how fine a television set may be, it will produce neither a clear picture nor sound without proper tuning. If one's faith is even slightly misdirected, he cannot fully realize his potential, nor will others follow him. Don't be overly concerned about this, however. Just sincerely practice the guidance you receive. The human mind is far more intricate than the finest television.

An individual who is out of rhythm with the organization is like a 33 r.p.m. record played at 45 r.p.m.

Profound delight

There is no end to human skepticism. Conviction means to make the supreme Law your basis and practice it with the confidence that your goals will definitely be realized. Then good results will naturally come about. This is the mysterious function of a person's *Ichinen.* One's *Ichinen* determines both happiness and unhappiness. Happiness cannot be judged by externals but depends solely on your *Ichinen* and good fortune.

A passage from the *Gosho* states, *Because all life is nothing more than Ichinen, the Buddha explains the benefits of profound delight (Ichinen Zuiki).* Thus Buddhism explains that *Ichinen* is life itself. *Ichinen* does not refer to something purely spiritual but penetrates the realm of *Shiki Shin Funi. Profound delight* in this *Gosho* means the joy one experiences at fusing his *Ichinen* with the supreme Law. When he carries this joyous spirit into his Gakkai activities, he receives both material and spiritual benefits.

↭

It's important to enjoy your practice. That's why you should treasure the unity of Sokagakkai members as though it were your personal possession. Even one negative individual can cause unpleasantness for all.

It is vital to create, through mutual understanding, an environment where everyone can enjoy activities even when faced with hardships. This is important in your daily life too. Let's strive to construct a bright, pure world where people can trust one another.

Rules

Faith means to tap your inherent Buddhahood through chanting Daimoku and doing Shakubuku. Fusing your life with the Gohonzon *(Kyochi Myogo)* will activate the life of the Gohonzon within you, bringing out your own *enlightenment.* If you hold grudges or feel hatred towards others, or if you are conceited, you cannot reveal your innate condition of Buddhahood.

In baseball, certain rules must be followed. A player would be laughed at if he hit the ball and ran straight from home plate to third base.

Maybe you can laugh off the small problems around you. But in the course of our lives, many things lie ahead which we cannot see. However, an absolute law of life is definitely operating there. People fail and become unhappy because they are out of rhythm with this law. Even if you embrace the Gohonzon and practice Buddhism, if you criticize or nurture ill feelings toward others, you will fall out of rhythm with this law and no longer receive benefits.

The rising sun

Because the struggle for Kosen-rufu is a long one, you may get tired or discouraged. Yet at other times, you may be filled with joy or burning conviction. As ordinary human beings, we experience various life-conditions, just as there are snowy, rainy and clear days. Yet as long as the sun rises, the sky will eventually clear, and as long as you have faith, you will ultimately become happy. Faith is having the confidence that you can change your own destiny.

When we're tired or discouraged, let's encourage each other. This is unity in a nutshell. To establish *enlightenment* in this lifetime and attain

Kosen-rufu, we must forge a pure and indestructible unity, embracing the Gohonzon till the end.

The true aspect of life

Faith reveals the true aspect of life. Regardless of how much one may rationalize or speak beautiful words, they amount to no more than cheap tactics. The proof of the pudding is in the eating. What counts is the "true aspect" of the present moment and the *Ichinen* underlying it. Excuses are unnecessary.

Breaking deadlocks

Hosshaku Kempon means to replace theory with practice. Carrying out your determination equals *Hosshaku Kempon*. Whenever you come to a stalemate, achieve *Hosshaku Kempon*. Every time you achieve *Hosshaku Kempon,* at that moment, your faith will advance. This is what Buddhism calls the "valiant and untiring practice" *(Yumyo Shojin)*.

Falling behind

When you realize you're lagging behind the progress of the organization, you can make fresh progress from that moment. When an individual feels satisfied, he can't advance. Top senior leaders, upon returning from a guidance tour, make it a point to immediately catch up on the progress of the organization. This reflects their faith and development.

Chapter Four: Practice

Adversity

Sincerity and insincerity are like two sides of the same coin. One may "praise the supreme teaching (*Honmon*) yet cherish transient teachings (*Shakumon*) in his heart." Nothing is so subtle as a man's mind.

People show their true colors when they are hard pressed in a life-or-death crisis. One could say that when Akechi Mitsuhide[1] raised the banner of revolt against his lord, Oda Nobunaga, the thoughts that had lain hidden in his heart emerged, triggered by circumstance.

You can gauge a person's true value according to how he struggles in times of adversity. For example, you can tell what is truly in the heart of a Sokagakkai leader when he is stripped of his position. Does he continue his practice to the Gohonzon and sincerely follow the organization, or not?

Buddhism means to base one's life on the master-disciple relationship. For a disciple, no act carries heavier consequences than betraying his master's trust.

---

[1] Akechi Mitsuhide—chief retainer of Oda Nobunaga, who held a grudge against his lord. When Nobunanga's top general and many of his troops were away on campaign, Mitsuhide murdered Nobunaga. Was later killed by Hideyoshi.

A sense of purpose

One who takes heartfelt responsibility for his members' happiness and guides them accordingly is truly a great person. If you are always elated about your activities at one moment and deadlocked or spiritless the next, it could be because your practice is still self-centered.

Naturally, I have bad days too. But if I were constantly up and down, in high spirits on some days and dejected on others, I'd feel sorry for the members. Human beings are weak. They become strong, however, when they live with a sense of purpose. Strength depends on one's *Ichinen* to practice.

Positive spirit

When you practice this Buddhism with a positive, seeking mind, you will receive benefits and improve your life. If you have a passive attitude, however, you'll tend to feel pressured or resentful. You will lose your inspiration to practice, gain fewer benefits and be led by force of habit.

Acting positively with the confidence that everything is for your own growth constitutes the true practice of Buddhism.

In a fundamental sense, embracing the Gohonzon is in itself the most positive action there is. Even Sakyamuni's closest disciples, Kasho and Anan, could not appear in this time of Mappo because they feared hardships. Now that you are practicing, you needn't worry about being passive.

Fame

Nothing passes so quickly as fame, yet people still frantically pursue such vain illusions. To a man who lives for honor alone, life will be over when his honor is lost. A man who seeks only others' approval will feel worthless when he loses his popularity. One who wields power over others will be toppled by it, and a man who values wealth above everything will be shattered when his wealth is gone.

Our campaign, based on the supreme Buddhism of Nichiren Daishonin, will never be destroyed. It is the ultimate good—the most meaningful struggle.

Faith cannot be seen

You can read what is written on paper, but some things cannot be expressed in words. Such things are hard to feel or grasp. You can see Nam-myoho-renge-kyo inscribed on the Gohonzon, but the meaning of faith is not something that can be explained on paper. The important thing is to experience a realization for yourself.

Decisive battle each day

Every day is a series of decisive battles. Success won yesterday won't necessarily guarantee success today. Likewise, just because yesterday may have gone badly doesn't mean today must go badly too. What counts is our moment-by-moment struggle. The sum of each moment's victory or defeat is reflected in our wisdom and good fortune and eventually becomes the balance sheet of our entire lives.

Obstacles

It's easy to drive when the road is clear, but it won't improve your skill as a driver. This holds true with our practice, too. Unless obstacles challenge you at every turn, you cannot change your destiny for the better.

A camera

No matter how fine a camera you may have, it's useless unless you open the shutter. In the same way, you won't gain from listening to guidance unless you earnestly try to absorb it and put it into practice.

Among those people who chant to the Gohonzon, some receive benefits and develop their lives, while others don't progress as rapidly or receive the benefits that they could. The difference is a matter of who makes willing efforts to practice the guidance they receive.

A camera holds only a narrow strip of film, yet it can reproduce a broad landscape or a large group of people. This instrument was devised by man, a product of his *Ichinen*. Through our *Ichinen*, too, we can be aware of all the ever-changing feelings of other people, the details of our huge organization and the affairs of the entire world.

Practice

The finest blueprint is useless by itself. Without a power source, the best machinery won't run. Even a good TV set won't project an image unless you turn on the electricity. In the same way, no matter how much deep theory you expound, it's not faith unless you back it up with practice.

Some people scale mountains confidently, even without knowing the theory of mountain-climbing. If you're captivated by theory but don't balance it with practice, you cannot benefit from faith.

Work and Gakkai activities

Establishing a balance between work and Gakkai activities is a problem everyone experiences at some time. When one of your members has this problem, first of all, simply listen to him so you can understand his situation, even if it seems as though he's just complaining. Then, depending on the individual, you can guide him in one of three directions.

The first is to have him concentrate on his job and chant Daimoku courageously. The second is to encourage him to strive hard at both work and activities. The third is to give him direct guidance on faith itself.

After carefully considering each aspect—his job situation, the strength of his faith, his living conditions and so forth—give him concrete guidance he can accept.

At times when you cannot go to meetings, what counts is your faith and *Ichinen*. Buddhism explains that cause and effect are simultaneous (*Inga Guji*), so in time, your strong desire alone will enable you to freely participate in activities. After maintaining this determination for a year or two, you will see results without fail. However, if you use your job as an excuse and think casually, "It's okay, then, I don't have to go," you will never improve your destiny.

※

Once you make the Gohonzon your basis, you will clearly perceive the law of cause and effect. Cause and effect governs all of human life, but because your destiny, your past causes, the strength of your practice and countless other factors are intricately woven together, it is difficult to attribute a particular effect to one specific cause. However, you will fully grasp the workings of causality through actual proof from the Gohonzon. A sincere practice is like a mirror of yourself, giving you your own standard to live by.

Youth is the time to build your foundation. You can't build a house if you lose your initiative or give up before completing the foundation.

Most people would rather go their own way than seek guidance. But the youth who considers himself free and easy is like a kite with its string cut. He will lose out later. While young, you must be passionate and ambitious in order to develop yourself.

Construction and regression

Gakkai members are strong in the face of hardships but vulnerable in the world of *rapture*. Never forget the early days of your faith and strive continuously with the spirit of Buddhist practice. Construction is difficult, but regression is swift.

A stupid person tries to make himself look big and lord it over others. Nothing is so fearful as a man's mind.

Precaution

These are the keys to our faith:

1. Every day, resolve that "I will start from now" with the spirit of *Hon'in-myo*.

2. Every day, keep faith with the spirit that "now is my last moment."

3. Every day, do your best so you will have no regrets.

It is said that "precaution will save a country from ruin" or "Care prevents accidents." But many businesses have failed and many nations have fallen, even with the greatest precautions. In the end, the final key to precaution is to realize that faith equals daily life. True precaution is our faith itself.

───

Whether or not you can maintain real happiness day by day depends solely on your faith. It's important to take a good look at yourself, reminding yourself, "I've got to remember this" or "I'd better straighten up," and prepare for tomorrow with the spirit of *Hon'in-myo*. Demons dwell in the world of *rapture*. When you relax in your practice and can't recognize them, you will suffer defeat.

Commitment

"Nam" of Nam-myoho-renge-kyo means to return your life to the Gohonzon and stand by that commitment no matter what. This doesn't mean you should have a fatalistic feeling. Wholehearted commitment to the practice means that we become fully confident of the Gohonzon's benefits, enjoy our lives and acquire absolute happiness.

Fortune

Fortune is the basis of happiness. No matter how bright you are or how excellent your upbringing, without fortune, you will be unhappy. Now, in Mappo, there is absolutely no other source of good fortune than chanting Nam-myoho-renge-kyo.

Once you gain fortune, everything else follows, according to the principle of *Esho Funi*. Your life broadens. You feel happy. Even your appearance changes. Your relations with others become as warm and open as a spring sky. Everything will change to happiness for you. It is vital to live with the confidence that you are definitely accumulating fortune for yourself.

School and Gakkai activities

For some students, studying and Gakkai activities conflict. Worrying about it will not help. Faith is our basis; we can practice it no matter where we are. Former President Josei Toda carried out the true practice of Buddhism in prison.

He attained *enlightenment* there, and even urged the jailors to practice.

College lasts four years, but faith and Gakkai activities are a lifetime campaign. Faith is eternal and right now, your student life itself is faith. While you're in school, make your faith the driving force of your studies and advance with the determination to become the best student possible.

Faith is your foundation and study is your main task, so Gakkai activities may have to be subordinate for now. Even so, you'll lose your spirit if you just do school work without participating in any activities. Therefore, I suggest you go to at least some meetings during the month. Other than that, use your own common sense to organize your life.

Mission

Everyone inherently possesses a mission. Chant Daimoku, receive training and live up to the mission you must ultimately achieve. Everyone who practices true Buddhism has a mission to fulfill. Right now you can also be confident of your mission as a leader in the Sokagakkai. If you advance with a burning sense of mission, the future will open up for you without fail.

Gakkai activities

Gakkai activities become meaningful when you do them voluntarily. That is the Buddhist practice today. The pre-Lotus Sutra teachings of *Shakumon* preached an individualized practice, benefitting only oneself. However, a self-centered intellectual lost in metaphysical abstractions cannot help anyone change his destiny.

In the *Honmon* teachings, the moment one determines to practice, his whole condition changes from *Tokaku* to *Myokaku*. Though his actions are those of a Bodhisattva, his life is fundamentally that of Buddha; he is concerned not only for himself but for other people's happiness. So long as we act with only the Sokagakkai in mind, we are still practicing *Shakumon*. We must launch our campaign toward the happiness of society, our homeland and the world.

First President Makiguchi, used to say, "It's all right to be scolded for a mistaken action. But it's bad to be scolded for taking no action."

You receive benefits when you voluntarily decide to practice for Kosen-rufu.

The thing to remember in doing Gakkai activities is "don't stop the engine." When your car engine dies, it's troublesome to start it up again. A writer who sets his manuscript aside finds it harder and harder to resume writing. It's important to keep a steady rhythm of activities, always following the organization.

Daimoku

How much Daimoku you chant is a matter of your own self-awakening. Chanting Daimoku is the foundation of happiness and of material and spiritual growth.

Daimoku is the source of development. In order to lead your members, you yourself must chant more Daimoku than they do. Unless you feel that you've got to study harder and continually develop yourself, your members won't progress. This is the law of consistency from beginning to end (*Honmatsu Kukyo-to*).

A million Daimoku won't improve your life if you hold doubts or merely chant out of formality. But when you yourself set a goal and chant for it, everything in life will open up to you. Even tens of millions of Daimoku chanted mechanically or grudgingly will not help you to break a deadlock.

Overdoing it

You must practice assiduously, but you should not overreach yourself or put on a false show.

Just because someone wealthier than you buys a new car for activities, you needn't feel you must too. That would be unreasonable. Doing your best in Shakubuku within your present limits constitutes *Zuiriki Enzetsu*.

Sometimes a person will immediately pass on the guidance he's just received to others before he's digested it himself. This also is overreaching oneself.

Faith equals daily life

Because cause and effect are simultaneous (*Inga Guji*), your morning Gongyo determines your whole day. When you do a strong, sincere morning Gongyo, your whole day is secure, consistent with the principle of consistency from beginning to end. Likewise, your prayer and determination during evening Gongyo—"Let me fight vigorously tomorrow too"— will decide the next day's results. This is the true practice of "faith equals daily life."

When you fail, "change poison into medicine" (*Hendoku Iyaku*) and start fighting again for your goal. This is value creation in the truest sense. Don't just flaunt your own ability. The wisest course of action is to share your dream with your juniors, harmonize their efforts, educate them, train them and advance with them, side by side.

Purification

The torrent thundering over a waterfall flows so swiftly that any debris is swept away. Discarded garbage rots in the stagnant waters of the Sumida River and pollutes the surroundings. Mountain streams quickly purify themselves of waste; their currents are bubbling and clear.

You may be troubled a bit by *Sansho Shima*. But so long as your faith wells up continuously like a mountain spring, you can defeat them all.

The Sokagakkai, too, so long as we progress with resolute faith, will naturally sweep aside all obstacles that challenge it. We must advance like the torrent of a great river, refusing to let it stagnate.

Self-awakening

Your self-awakening will open a whole new future. In the Gakkai, those who have been appointed senior leaders and awakened to their mission and responsibility are now developing splendidly. This is proof of their faith.

When you perceive you are a *Jiyu-no Bosatsu*, you can manifest the power of *Jiyu-no Bosatsu*. When you are aware of yourself as a member of the Sokagakkai, your faith is progressing. A member of the Senate may also experience this self-awakening. When he is constantly aware that he must carry out the tasks of a senator, his ability emerges. His position as senator is "law," and his awakening to his own responsibility as a senator is "person." Together, they compose the principle of oneness of person and law (*Ninpo Ikka*).

Contemporary politicians have no such insight

or awareness, so there is no fusion of law and person.

The Sokagakkai must not be colored by one man's personality. The vitality of the organization stems from the vibrant lives of all the members. This is why we appear conservative to some and progressive to others. Buddhism is the all-encompassing teaching (*Enkyo*), so they are both correct.

Master and disciple

For one man alone to become great is the way of a dictator. Because a dictator himself is intrinsically weak, he wields power and wealth to prove how strong he is and looks down on others as fools.

Buddhism means the inseparability of master and disciple (*Shitei Funi*). This is fundamentally different from a dictatorship. The master lets his disciples share the same task and the same *enlightenment* with him equally. This is true democracy. A central figure is necessary, however, in accordance with the principle of *Kutai Kuyu*.

The master strives to raise his disciples to his own level and then even higher. This is the fundamental difference between the world of Buddhism, or the Sokagakkai, and the rest of society. Because we are raising so many committed leaders, others tend to conclude that we are deliberately creating factions. But our action is based upon faith. It is precisely because we are developing new leaders that we can make such wide-range, magnificent progress, unequalled by other organizations.

I have never said that you are disciples nor that I am the master. I feel that under the Gohonzon we are all equal, all disciples of former President Toda, the master of Shakubuku. But, I hope you'll forge ahead joyfully and feel confident that the President is taking the lead in our organization's great objective of Kosen-rufu.

We are not talking about the mere formality of saying, "I'm his disciple" or "He is my master." The master-disciple relationship is much deeper, arising from your own self-awakening.

I traveled the road of master and disciple with former President Toda for ten years. I resolved that even if my master should fall into hell, I would run to his side. I would commit my life to this, and even if I were deluded I didn't care, so long as I was with my master. This, I decided, was the bond between master and disciple.

Gongyo

Your crisp tone of voice and precise rhythm in doing Gongyo express your confidence. Your faith shows when you chant too loudly or too softly, or don't clearly pronounce the words. Gongyo is the foundation of everything, so you must do it correctly.

High spirits

No matter how well your group is organized, you'll be defeated if your spirits aren't high. With high spirits, you can win in anything.

High spirits can be called synonymous with faith, vitality, rhythm and harmony. History, social movements and election campaigns of the past all bear this out.

Faith without doubt

Faith means having no doubts. This is called *Mugi Wasshin*. Merely chanting Daimoku in a loud voice doesn't mean you have strong faith.

No matter what happens, don't doubt the Gohonzon. Keep faith as the Daishonin directed and follow the Sokagakkai. This is *Mugi Wasshin*, the ultimate result of faith.

One who immediately starts doubting or criticizing or whose confidence is shaken as soon as something goes wrong can never be considered a man of strong faith.

Criticizing

A person advancing in his practice does not criticize others. Instead, he is concerned and understanding. The man who criticizes only shows that his faith is stagnant, that he has lost sight of his goal and is making no progress.

Even a person with a weak or twisted nature can elevate his life through strong Daimoku. When one does nothing but criticize, he acts as a devil.

A man may slander the Gohonzon and seem

not to suffer for it, but it's only temporary. From a short-sighted viewpoint, there may indeed be cases like this. But life is long, and you should observe the whole course of his life before you judge.

In another sense, you can't really judge until you see a man's last moments. Not even one person who spoke ill of the Gohonzon or betrayed the Sokagakkai ever became happy.

On the other hand, those who have continued practicing in spite of many troubles for ten or fifteen years have achieved great strides in their human revolution and transformed their daily lives. They are now the top leaders of the Sokagakkai. You can never judge the supreme Law of Buddhism by temporary phenomena or surface appearances.

The emcee

When the emcee addresses a discussion meeting, he should think of it as a battlefield. He should burn with the resolve to transform it into the Buddha's land (*Jakko-do*).

Even if the speaker fails, or if the room becomes too noisy, the emcee should have the conviction to steer the meeting back on course. He must consider this his responsibility and be able to carry it out.

He wins when he considers the meeting his

own battleground, harmonizing the mood of the people there and creating an elated atmosphere. When he cannot do this, he fails. The emcee determines victory or defeat for the entire meeting.

Those who live by faith

A monkey, even if he falls out of a tree, is still a monkey. But a senator is not a senator if he loses the election. So long as you practice you can reach *enlightenment*, but if you lose your faith you will be in *hell*.

Large financial concerns may have ample funds, but because of today's fluctuating business conditions, they confront an extremely trying economic situation. They suffer precisely because they have money. Once a famous man loses his fame, people won't stop to glance at him. The world can be cold and ruthless. The only real treasure in life is faith.

Famous people are not necessarily happy. Looking closely, one sees they are all troubled. Baseball players, movie stars — simply because they've become famous, others look up to them as somebody special. This makes them conceited. You need a correct basis for judgment to see things clearly. This is vital in everything and becomes possible only through faith.

People who rise in the world through money become arrogant because they have money and fall into hell over money. People who float through life on their fame are ruined by it and suffer when their popularity fails. Those who gain status by power are overthrown by power. Only those who live by faith can live peacefully always, neither defeated nor ruled by anything.

When one embraces the Gohonzon, his destructive attitudes toward people, society and the world will disappear. He won't want to hate, kill or deceive others. Quite naturally, his life will become as harmonious and perfect as a full moon. He can hold a correct view of people, society and daily life, oriented toward creating peace and happiness. To chant Daimoku to the Gohonzon is to lead the true way of life.

Attaining enlightenment

Because we are human, we may sometimes get sick. It's important to have the faith that "even if I am poisoned, I will never doubt the Gohonzon."

Even if you get robbed or have a traffic accident, be confident that the Gohonzon's benefit is absolute. This is true faith. One who is swayed by immediate gain or loss forgets the great objective and becomes ensnared in superficial problems.

The purpose of our practice is to attain *enlightenment* in this life (*Issho Jobutsu*). We can do this only through embracing the Gohonzon. Because Buddhism explains that an effect is inherent within its cause (*Inga Guji*), embracing the Gohonzon is itself equal to *enlightenment*. This is called *Juji soku Kanjin*. In concrete terms, this means to make faith our basis, follow the Gakkai till the last moment and enjoy our lives through tapping our inner wellspring of vitality. Practice hard so you will have no regrets. In faith, schemes are unnecessary.

Two principles often mentioned in the *Gosho* are: *One who chants even one Daimoku will gain immense fortune*, and *Even if you profess faith, if your faith is weak, you cannot reach*

enlightenment and you will fall into hell at your dying moment. People frequently wonder if these aren't contradictory.

The explanation is this: Suppose a man has been hired by a publishing firm. Because he's an employee, he is entitled to receive a paycheck. But subsequently, if he doesn't work hard or develop in his position, his salary may be cut or he may get fired or demoted to a degrading position. His suffering and loneliness then are truly *hell*.

So long as you chant Daimoku, you are qualified to attain *enlightenment*. You cannot do so, however, unless you carry out a lifetime practice of Buddhism as the Daishonin taught. Chanting one Daimoku implants the cause for *enlightenment* in your life, but to establish eternal and absolute happiness, you must practice Buddhism.

Smooth sailing

Right now, the Sokagakkai is like a ship sailing before the wind. An old saying goes, "Pride goeth before a fall." We must never become like this. Even while things are going smoothly, we should consider the worst that could happen and economize in everything. Otherwise, we won't continue for very long.

Members of society

Gakkai members should all be excellent citizens as well as followers of Nichiren Daishonin's true Buddhism. The Daishonin explained that Buddhism encompasses all other phenomena. He demonstrated that faith itself is the basis for making politics, economics, education and all other aspects of culture flourish. For this reason, Gakkai members should become more respectworthy members of society than anyone else. With this strong conviction, excel above others at your job and win the trust and respect of your associates.

In society, you should never take advantage of the organization's influence or be arrogant. Whether in the world of Buddhism or among society, the actions of Gakkai members should set an example. With this awareness, you must act responsibly.

Instinct

We are instinctively seeking happiness, just as grass and trees thirst for the sun. People's lives have fallen into the suffering of the *three evil paths,* the *four lower worlds* and the cycle of the six worlds *(Rokudo Rinne).* When you stay in an outhouse for a long time, you stop noticing the stench. People who live in misery long enough stop thinking about trying to change it. Instinctively, however, everyone longs for indestructible happiness.

Human desires have no limits. People want to be richer or more famous or more intelligent, and so on. This, too, is instinctive and natural. Many times, though, people torture themselves with their desires and make themselves miserable. The fulfillment of all desire expounded by Buddhism is a crucial point.

Some people insist they're not looking for personal satisfaction. But in the depths of their hearts, they too are seeking happiness. Buddhism expounds nothing extraordinary; it clarifies the original and supreme of Law of the universe. From the standpoint of Buddhism's life-philosophy, man's search for happiness is instinctive.

Nature

There is a Buddhist saying: *"Nature is that which does not alter throughout the three existences."* Your fundamental nature is unchanging. For example, compare your life to a river. Its width does not broaden nor narrow appreciably. This corresponds to your unchanging nature. Your human revoulution and transformation of destiny, based on your faith, will decide whether the river is muddy or clear.

Your practice will not change your nature, such as your gentleness or strength of character, but it will perfect it. This is the process of achieving human revolution and changing your destiny.

Age

People should live healthy, enjoyable lives brimming with vitality. One's age is determined by how meaningfully he has lived. No matter how long he lives, a man who is always ill in bed is like a living corpse.

The measure of a man's true age is how much he has accomplished, which constitutes his worth as a human being.

The day after the storm

Be careful when your illness takes a turn for the worse. Don't let yourself be defeated at this time, either by your illness or by your own weakened spirit. Surmounting this crisis is a fight with the devil of sickness.

The day following a storm is always clear. After courageously breaking through a period of real suffering, you will feel refreshed and exhilarated. In defeating obstacles or devils, you will reach a higher stage of life. This is the mystic, fundamental law of Buddhism.

Democracy

I hear that from the outside, the Sokagakkai seems cold and strict. When you enter it, however, you will find that no other world is so free, so bright and so at ease. In the end, no other world is so democratic. Society, on the other hand, which appears to be free, is actually corrupt or feudalistic in many areas. The difference between the two worlds is the difference between what is superficial and what is real.

Diplomacy

Former President Toda used to say, "I cannot use a man with no sales talent or diplomacy."

Neither Hitler nor Hideki Tojo[1] ever left their native countries. For this reason, perhaps, they were unable to formulate diplomatic policy from a truly worldwide perspective. Instead, they became complacent and were ruined.

From now on, diplomacy will gradually supplant military strength. Rather than confining ourselves to a narrow view of the world, shouldn't we be striving to increase our knowledge and broaden our horizons?

A diary

Whether we keep a journal or not, our day-by-day actions are a diary recorded in gold letters. Memories of seeing a movie or of other amusements are as fragile as bubbles.

As long as we live, we want to leave behind us memories of the many great campaigns we fought for Kosen-rufu. Young people especially

---

[1] Hideki Tojo—Japan's prime minister during WW II. Executed as a war criminal in 1946.

should live so that when they open their diary of gold letters in the future, they will not find even a single blank page.

Arrogance

In examining yourself, ask yourself if you're capable or not, if you're developing or not, or if you even know yourself. Think about it carefully. Conceit is common to all human beings. Eight out of ten people are destroyed by their own arrogance.

Doctorate

Even if you cannot go to school, that's all right, if you carry out your human revolution. Your human revolution is the important thing.

Don't downgrade yourself. A person who has confidence in the Gohonzon is far greater than a man with a Ph.D. who can't accept Buddhism. In the Sokagakkai today, old people, young people, men and women are all earnestly studying the supreme philosophy of Buddhism. No other group studies as hard as ours. We should strive to earn an invisible doctorate in absolute happiness.

One who studies the supreme philosophy and

has found the road to ultimate happiness should be called a great scholar. Make a determination to show others that even though you didn't go to school, you still became a person of value. There are many capable men taking an active role in society who never went to school. There is no reason why young people who are practicing Buddhism can't become even greater.

People of few words

Shyness could be called an inherent trait. However, you can achieve a remarkable human revolution through your practice. Because you're changing your destiny, you can actually become eloquent. Even many senior leaders were once very quiet. Eloquence doesn't mean mere fluency of speech or frivolous chatter. You should become someone who can speak confidently and to the point when you must give guidance.

Trust

Former President Toda used to tell us, "The important thing in youth is not honor or position or property. In your youth, you must gain the trust of others."

While you're young, you needn't worry over money. Consider your own development as your greatest wealth.

Society

Developing an eye to judge people requires many repetitions of trial and error in real situations.

Someone once complained, "Even though I'm young, I have to deal with seasoned businessmen. If I don't stand firm, they cheat me right and left."

In the end, "faith first" is the basis of everything. When you practice with determination, you are definitely protected by the *Shoten Zenjin*, who will shield you from underhanded schemes.

The cleverness of an evil man is a perverse talent developed through subterfuge. He is always watching for the opportunity to take advantage of others. Our wisdom originates from faith. When you're growing in your practice, you will naturally be able to make timely judgments and forestall failure.

Sometimes people make errors in judgment because they take their own opinion as their sole criterion. Consult with your seniors and listen carefully to what they say. Checking your views in the light of theirs will help you to make the best decision.

The way of youth

Young people must not be weak-spirited. Because you're human, you'll have troubles. Summon up your courage and fight them.

Don't keep your problems to yourself, though. If you talk with your seniors, they can give you some suggestions to help you find a solution.

◦~◦~◦

Set a target for what you should be accomplishing right now. The task at hand has first priority. The rest will follow naturally. In the course of completing a project, you will come to understand your strong points and learn through observing your seniors. This is the road to your self-perfection.

Concern for your parents

If you live far from your parents, it's considerate on your part to send them something every month or two, if you can. Or, write them and let them know that you're well and working hard. Parents naturally worry about their children. A cheerful letter will put their minds at ease. This is one way of showing you care for them.

The greatest act of love you can show your parents is to enable them to chant to the Gohonzon. If they cannot chant, you should chant Daimoku for them. If your parents are deceased, you should chant Daimoku for their *enlightenment.*

Going abroad

If you have a dream to go to other countries, don't just passively think, "Well, maybe in a few years I can go." Decide that within so many years you will go for sure and start working toward that goal.

In the past, millions of young people went abroad in wartime as messengers of hell, bringing grief to the people of foreign countries. From now on, if many people go abroad as envoys of Buddhism, Sakyamuni, T'ien-t'ai and the True Buddha of Mappo, Nichiren Daishonin, will rejoice with all their hearts.

We must end the age of racial discrimination. This requires worldwide democracy. People everywhere are the same; a human being is a human being, no matter where he comes from. But to materialize this idea, the people of the world must join together in unity based on Buddhism of the Three Great Secret Laws. Without trust, people start doubting each other and creating friction. There's no end to it.

Live powerfully

Youth should eat, sleep well and work hard. You should carry out each day's work with burning passion.

Unless you take responsibility for the task at hand and resolve to accomplish it at all cost, you cannot lead others.

Young people should live powerfully. If you don't chant Daimoku with guts and develop your capability, no one will follow you.

Chapter Five: Hope

Hopes

Youth is the time to cherish great hopes. Yet those who fulfill their hopes are few indeed. Usually people's dreams fade as they approach middle age and disappear entirely by the time they are old. Faith is the confidence that you can live your life according to your greatest hopes.

One who hangs on to his hope until his last moment is happy. One who keeps fighting to realize it is great. Kosen-rufu and the prosperity of mankind based on a correct ideology are hopes, too.

Lenin once said, "Revolution is hope." But the only revolution that can fundamentally change anything is a revolution of values, basing every aspect of society upon absolute respect for human life. The construction of world peace depends on it. I hope you understand that we cannot realize this dream without the Gohonzon.

Deadlock

Buddhism is boundless. You should not be swayed by circumstances or entangled in your problems. No matter what the situation, if you practice, you can break your deadlock.

Didn't Hideyoshi Toyotomi[1] start out as an

---

[1] Toyotomi Hideyoshi—see footnote on page 115.

orderly? So long as we practice Buddhism, there's no limit to what we can accomplish. Faith is being able to act as we wish, regardless of our situation.

It is hardly surprising when an intelligent, healthy and well-educated man achieves prominence. It's much rarer for someone who has neither money nor an academic background. Through your practice, however, you can overcome such disadvantages and become an excellent person. That is your human revolution. This is the guidance of former President Toda and the teachings of Buddhism.

Life is like the race between the tortoise and the hare. The hare doesn't necessarily win. Even in the Sokagakkai, many leaders who never went to college give guidance to college graduates, helping them to become happy. This is the world of Buddhism.

Overcoming your circumstances

A person with no confidence in his own actions is unhappy. Life is a struggle for survival.

You should act confidently and without hesitation.

⚘

No matter where they grow, plants absorb water and nourishment in their thirst to live. An abandoned puppy will try to hunt in order to survive. This is a fundamental law of nature. Everything depends on whether you win or lose in the battle for survival. To achieve happiness, practice hard and develop the strength you need to win in life.

The purpose of faith is to overcome your present situation and enjoy your life until the last moment. He who is defeated by his surroundings and complains is a straggler in life.

⚘

Attaining *enlightenment* is not determined by whether your circumstances are good or bad. Former President Toda achieved *enlightenment* in prison, under the worst conditions imaginable.

While you are young, you should not be concerned about leading a comfortable life right away. Fight through your present circumstances to develop your capability and strength of character. Your struggles in times of hardship will become your most priceless memories later on.

Work while you're young

There is a saying, "Life is another name for struggle." And another, "Youth is the time for construction." It is also the time for training. Work and study as hard as you can while you are young.

The harder you work, the greater your hopes will become. We can see this in those who practice Buddhism. Live constructively, and in time, you can enjoy life more than anyone else.

Sleeping hours

When you wake up refreshed and in high spirits, even though you've slept a comparatively short time, it shows your life is in the right rhythm.

Life is wondrous. It provokes many questions that science and medicine cannot answer. Ultimately, it is a matter of *Ichinen*. For example, in the midst of a heavy campaign, we may hardly get any sleep, but we can still stay healthy and carry out vigorous activities. However, you should use common sense.

You are slandering Buddhism if you cause an accident through lack of sleep and create trouble for other people. Dozing off at important meetings also shows that your practice is slipping.

―――

Both Napoleon and Edison were careful to get enough sleep. A person who can't get adequate sleep will be miserable. He cannot be active in anything.

―――

People of ancient times created truly excellent art, partially, perhaps, because they had no electric lights and could sleep as much as they needed to. In any case, sleep is more beneficial than food.

Pursuing a rainbow

Creativity is the treasure of your twenties. You always should live youthfully and intensely. It's wonderful to live as though you were pursuing a rainbow.

Young people should not be slaves to money, prestige or other passing things. Stand tall, live proudly and fight for your goal. This doesn't mean you should deny reality. Unless you plant both feet firmly on the ground, you'll never even see that rainbow.

One who lives with a dream is happy. Our dreams must be directly linked to our faith. Now we are accomplishing Kosen-rufu, the dream of 700 years. When you think about it, isn't this a rainbow, too?

Eloquence

Through speaking in front of people, time after time, you'll become good at it naturally. Our meetings are not speech contests, however, nor are we professional storytellers. Our eloquence lies in encouraging others for the sake of Kosen-rufu. Sincerely praising the Gohonzon is the height of eloquence.

It is said that the most eloquent speech ever made was a three-minute address by a general in ancient Italy. The speech-making of contemporary politicians is like an oratorical contest among parrots. Their words hold no conviction, no reasoning, no mercy. There is utterly no need for us to imitate them.

Second phase of life

The essential thing for a couple is to put their faith before anything else. After marriage, you enter the second phase of life, with the responsibility of caring for your wife and raising a family.

Strengthen your practice, accumulate fortune and serve the Gohonzon together till the last moment, like Shijo Kingo, Toki Jonin, Nanjo Tokimitsu and their wives. Both of you should resolve to create a happy family as an example for your members.

To be specific, you have both a financial and social responsibility. As a husband, you need the capacity to love and understand your wife and protect her and your children from hunger.

Understanding without faith

When you don't practice, although realizing that you should, this is called *Uge Mushin*. It may be because you're tired, acting out of habit or neglecting the things around you. Some people stumble into this pitfall repeatedly while they're young, but if you cut yourself off from the Sokagakkai, you'll just be lost in a spiritual maze. Benefits only come through following the organization, so persevere in your practice.

Living confidently

Sometimes you'll feel unsure of your actions. At those times, arouse your faith and advance with a confident *Ichinen*. Unless you face your obligations with the determination that "everything's fine," you cannot progress.

So long as you do nothing but scrutinize yourself, you are still controlled by earthly desires (*Bon'no*). Faith is to make these *Bon'no* a foundation for happiness, transforming them into *enlightenment (Bon'no soku Bodai)*.

First of all, start the day with the feeling that "everything's fine." Introspection is for the sake of progress. Where there is progress, *Bon'no soku Bodai* becomes possible. Actually, you cannot say, "Everything's fine" until the day of Kosenrufu, or until the moment of your *enlightenment*. But from your present standpoint, unless you have the confidence that you're making a full effort, as though this were the last moment of your life, you cannot experience the full benefit of the practice.

Power and wisdom

The supreme Law is the wellspring of power and wisdom. Faith, therefore, is your confidence and feeling of responsibility as a leader to fulfill your mission at all cost. No matter how intelligent you are, you cannot help others change their destiny or give them direction in faith with your talent alone. Give guidance others can relate to. You don't have to impress anyone.

Revolution of thought

From here on, leaders must be able to apply their wisdom appropriately according to the circumstances (*Zuien Shinnyo-no Chi*). It's important to consult with your seniors, but you should also be able to answer questions yourself without checking with them on every single point.

Faith is both wisdom and the creation of value. Your guidance must give your members confidence. From now on, strive to transform not only your character but also your way of thinking.

Composure and fortitude

Guidance once given to youth division leaders stressed the importance of "composure and fortitude." A central figure should not respond to each bad report he receives with a shocked, "Oh, no — that's terrible!" If he's so easily swayed by circumstances, he cannot be considered mature. Instead, he should clearly judge the situation and firmly encourage the person who reported it, saying, "Don't worry about it. We're going to keep fighting for our goal no matter what happens." This is composure. Once you decide, "I will die for the Gohonzon," you can always act with self-possession.

Fortitude is the strength of character to lead all the members. When they are harassed by others on account of their practice or when they start to doubt after reading criticism of the organization in newspapers or magazines, a leader with fortitude encourages them, saying, "Don't worry. Isn't this exactly what Nichiren Daishonin said would happen? What we're doing is right, and I'm going to go right on doing it."

Acting in a high-handed way that makes members shy away from you does not show fortitude. You should have enough faith and consideration to make them trust you and wholeheartedly follow you. Then you have true fortitude.

Capable men and bright women

A man must be powerful. You should live like a lion, the king of beasts. One who can fight through to the end is a man among men. You must be able to show results without fail.

Women should not be jealous or ill-natured. Nor is it good to be gloomy. It's important to become a bright, sincere and polished individual.

It is a great mistake to think that the Sokagakkai will develop through the dynamics of its organization. Our growth results with each person who frankly shares his wisdom and ability. Ultimately, it is a matter of humanism. A capable person is not made in one day.

I received training from former President Toda for ten years. Even now I think how strange it is that he died exactly ten years after telling me, "I will train you for ten years."

Brilliant students and capable men

One who was brilliant in school will not necessarily emerge brilliantly in society. So far, promising students are still receiving a conventional education, which seeks only to cram them full of information. Until we break with this trend, we cannot encourage people of true genius.

Today, it seems one's value is decided by which clique he belongs to or where he went to school. Often, no matter how hard he tries, a brilliant man cannot utilize his full ability because of financial or political pressure.

Your vitality and wisdom will emerge through your faith in the Gohonzon. This is true genius. Even with the Gohonzon, people naturally have different abilities, but because these differences reflect our true individuality, we should wholeheartedly respect them.

Standing alone

No matter what you're doing, do it yourself first. Don't depend on somebody else. It is *Zuitai* to be swayed by another's opinion. Youth should have the spirit of *Zuijii*, to stand alone.

Regardless of what others may do or say, you should insist, "This is traditional Gakkai spirit," and practice it. This is faith.

If you feel you've been injured because you came early while everyone else was late, this is *Zuitai*. A person to whom it is only proper and natural to be on time, even when others are late, is admirable.

Whether you gain or lose, accumulate fortune or become miserable, is all determined by your own practice. Therefore, you don't need a critic to tell you if you're practicing correctly.

Efforts

Anyone who achieved greatness made painstaking efforts. The young people today who so often think only of living comfortably or of having money are making a serious error, from the long-range view of life. They will inevitably fail in their forties or fifties.

To develop as a capable person, you should, first of all, become the best on your job. Regardless of their occupations, those who strive harder and fight through more hardships are victors. Your struggle may be inconspicuous, but your sincere co-workers will understand it, and you yourself will be secure in the knowledge of your efforts. This is the law of cause and effect.

Promising generation

For those Gakkai members who are striving earnestly in their practice and receiving training now, the future is filled with immense fortune. An egg, at the beginning, contains only a kind of fluid. But then eyes form, and a beak, and gradually a whole chick emerges. The youth of today are like *Hosu*, or young phoenixes. Through forming ties with good leaders who will scold or encourage them as needed, they will no doubt develop splendidly.

Who could have imagined the Sokagakkai of today in the early days of our organization? I was just following President Toda. I was convinced that Kosen-rufu would surely be realized some day, so long as he had the *Ichinen* to achieve it. As cause and effect are simultaneous, it was already determined at that time that I would be what I am today. This is the ultimate principle of *Ichinen Sanzen*.

Judgment

When someone offers a sincere suggestion that will create new value and benefit all concerned, you should accept it, regardless of what it will cost.

Someone else, however, may suggest something merely to impress people, or because his way will be less trouble, or for some other reason stemming from an irresponsible or selfish attitude. In this case, even if his idea is good, you should not adopt it until he changes his way of thinking.

Mission of youth

No matter what happens, I don't ever want you to experience war. It is my prayer and my resolve that people will walk in peace on the road toward happiness.

Men seriously concerned with the real problems of mankind are rare indeed. These earnest individuals have fallen by the wayside and in their place, egotistical malcontents exert their influence. We asked to be born at this time in order to achieve Kosen-rufu. The more hardships we confront, the more worthwhile our effort, don't you agree?

This task can only be achieved by youth. Therefore, we must bring together many young people and develop them, study together with them and train them to become great leaders who possess good fortune. In time, they will be making outstanding achievements in society as diplomats, scientists, artists and engineers.

I will open the road to Kosen-rufu. We must stop the nation from plunging into violence by all means. Also, I wish to convey the thoughts of former President Toda to the youth division. I hope you will become men of justice.

Youthfulness

Many people become settled in their ways after they marry and start a family. However, one who stops growing in his twenties or thirties is a failure as a human being.

First President Makiguchi was still studying English at seventy, just like a young man. Even when he was past sixty, he was the first to dive straight into the icy water of Shiraito Falls. Regardless of your age, you should never seem old or settled. Otherwise, you cannot take an active role as a world leader in the future.

Staying young depends solely on faith. Our bodies age, but through the *Ichinen* of faith, you can retain your youthfulness. It is a great man who maintains his youthful spirit throughout life.

On the job

Don't feel you have to dress up now, just because you've become a leader. A grocer should look like a grocer, and a factory worker, like a factory worker. What counts is working for all you're worth and becoming an example for others on your job. It is a great thing to take pride in your work and lead a life brimming with confidence.

Responsibility

It is wrong to jump to conclusions and give thoughtless guidance, just because you're busy. No matter what, you should put yourself in the other person's place, understand his situation fully and direct him with the feeling that his problems are your personal responsibility. Such awareness and sincerity are essential in a leader.

It is frightening that a leader, entrusted with the priceless lives of his members, would give them careless guidance. You should guide your members confidently and responsibly, with understanding and care.

"This time, no matter what..."

One who advances with perpetually fresh determination will achieve his human revolution without fail. One who feels "I'm already doing fine" is backsliding.

"This time, no matter what..." Making such determinations again and again is the faith of ordinary people. This is how we can realize our human revolution and establish strong faith. Many people, however, appear to have strong faith when actually they are just self-assertive. Mere self-assertiveness will definitely lead you into a stalemate. You should strengthen your faith.

Road of pioneers

Waves surge from the prow of a sailing ship and a car on the road raises dust. To live courageously as a pioneer, you must conquer many hardships.

Obstacles that arise on the road to Kosen-rufu can all be changed into causes for progress through *Hendoku Iyaku*.

Questions

A person who asks questions is progressing. It shows that he has a seeking mind. One who doesn't even have questions is passive and easily ruled by habit.

~~~

Live youthfully. You must have the energy to advance day by day, no matter what problems confront you. Since we are human beings, there are times when we act out of habit and times when we're down. But when it comes to Buddhism, be resolved to advance with a drive that will make sparks fly.

Chasing two hares

It is said that "If you run after two hares you will catch neither." However, if you are capable enough, you can chase and catch not only two hares, but even three or four.

Standard for disciples

The bond between master and disciple is the fundamental point of Buddhism. First President Makiguchi and second President Toda had this master-disciple relationship. A disciple must live up to strict standards.

First, he must absolutely never worry his master in the least.

Second, he must not make such mistakes as backsliding in his practice or misusing money.

Third, he must protect his master: financially, socially and in every way possible. You are not protecting your master — on the contrary, he protects you.

Fourth, he must practice everything his master says, without the least doubt or hesitation.

"Faith like snow"

Faith, a seeking mind and the Gakkai spirit are all the same thing. With "faith like snow," you will not hold grudges, feel jealous or criticize others. It is simply a pure, trusting relationship between you and the Gohonzon.

Everything works for your own *enlightenment*. Think of advice from your friends and seniors as something to help develop your faith. Regardless of whether you're praised or criticized, take it as the driving force of your practice. This is "faith like snow."

Good omens

One could say that because you protect the Gohonzon, this is proof that you and your family are protected by the *Shoten Zenjin*. According to the *Zuiso Gosho*, if you have faith, positive signs will definitely appear.

The law of causality becomes clear through your practice of the supreme Law. Because you chanted Daimoku in some past lifetime, you are able to practice today. Knowing this, you should be confident of your future this time.

Critics today take a narrow view of Buddhism, as though peering through the end of a straw. They cannot possibly grasp the Daishonin's supreme ideology. It is so far beyond their imagination they would be appalled. Unless one views Buddhism from the standpoint of five or ten years' practice, he has no basis for criticism.

⁓⁓⁓

Life is *Ichinen Sanzen,* with three thousand different dimensions. People's lives differ according to their destiny, cause-and-effect relationships, their surroundings, the depth of their faith and so on. Even among the simple relationships of cause and effect in society, there are many cases where one plus one does not necessarily equal two. This is even more fundamentally true in Buddhism, where a single moment contains all causes and effects throughout eternity. Obviously, it is not a simple matter.

The only important thing is to be confident and show results through your faith.

Nikko Shonin and the five main priests

Why did five of the six senior priests closest to the Daishonin betray him after his death? Those five did not remain continually at his side, and therefore failed to grasp his true intention. As they only came occasionally to hear him talk about the supreme Buddhism, it is not surprising that they did not comprehend.

Only Nikko Shonin, who served the Daishonin constantly, could understand his ultimate intention.

A majority decision, therefore, does not necessarily constitute democracy. Had it not been for Nikko Shonin alone, there would be no Nichirenshoshu today. I feel that the Sokagakkai itself is Nikko Shonin, and that the members who are doing Shakubuku and advancing together with the organization for the cause of Kosenrufu are Nikko Shonin, too.

Enjoyable practice of Buddhism

Faith means you should all unite joyfully. Because you are practicing Buddhism, however, you will also face hardships at times. In the ancient Buddhist practice, Gyobo Bonji removed his skin and copied a sutra on it. Bodhisattva Yakuo offered lights to the Buddha made by burning his own elbows. Sessen Doji sought *enlightenment* by offering his body to a demon.

Compared to these austerities, our own practice is extremely easy. You should practice as hard as you can and fight to achieve *enlightenment* in your lifetime *(Issho Jobutsu)*.

Work

Your own wisdom, awakened through faith, is the foundation for managing your business. But don't neglect study and hard work. If you think just chanting Daimoku is enough, you're mistaken.

You must consider your customers, know your rivals and keep your accounts in order. Otherwise, there is no way you can succeed.

❧

You should control your work, not let your work control you. If you lack initiative, or if your business doesn't inspire you, it shows you are being manipulated by your job.

When things get hectic, you may lose sight of the main point of your work. This, too, is letting your job rule you. When you are quite clear about what you should do, the responsibility you should take and the focus of your work, then you are in control of your job.

❧

Among those people dissatisfied with their work, some actually have unsatisfactory jobs, while others are defeated by their work and think that someone else's job must be better. Even if they change jobs, things will be the same until they win in their work. As a general rule, you should resolve to accumulate good fortune at your present job.

One who is trusted and respected at his job is ultimately a winner. Even if one practices Buddhism, if he forgets to study or work hard and leaves things half done, others will forsake him in the end. It is only natural that people should be eager to work. Each of you has your own mission and responsibility. You must develop the capability to carry it out.

To become the best person on your job is *Ninpo Ikka.* To neglect your work is *Ninpo Shoretsu.* If you expect to become a leader or hold a responsible position, it is only natural that you struggle tenaciously. On the other hand, if your company is within an inch of bankruptcy, the executives are incompetent, the future looks dark and collapse is clearly inevitable, then, you are free to go. You must not feel it is your destiny to strive at such a job, or that you are chained to it in any way.

Foresight, deliberation, resolve

The following three points are essential for a businessman.

First, he needs clear foresight, just as a politician must always keep one step ahead to judge how the times are changing and what measures he should adopt.

Second is thorough deliberation. Strategy is important in business. You should take into account the worst that could happen and consider things carefully from all possible angles.

Third is resolve. This means the ability to make a decision and act on it. Once you've decided something, no matter what happens, carry it out swiftly with the same determination as though you were breaking through a stone wall. This is what I mean by resolve.

In society

At the height of Napoleon's power, it is said that whenever he entered a room, all eyes would turn toward him simultaneously as though he glittered. This story reflects his charisma, dignity and vigor.

It also symbolizes the hero-worship and authoritarian outlook of the day. But it does suggest the distinguishing youthful aura, appearance and the kind of spark young Sokagakkai members should have.

In your social relations, you must always act with proper courtesy, dignity and charm. But in your heart, hold fast to your resolve to face your struggle. Young people need not be stiff or phony. All in all, it is best to be yourself.

If you act arrogantly in order to impress people, you won't succeed. You must equip yourself in a natural way, with strength, intelligence, dignity and the capacity for struggle.

Today a man is ridiculed who swaggers about with shoulders squared and chest outthrust as was fashionable earlier in the century. People's eyes are sharp. You must progress, developing your capability and character. This is what counts in the end.

Faith equals daily life

"Faith equals daily life" means to create value in your work. The benefits of faith emerge only through the *nine worlds* — that is, in your daily life. Showing the benefits of your practice in society is faith. Think of your job as the Gohonzon and become a winner there.

No matter what happens, you should never give up in your work or become a straggler on your job.

Regardless of your position in the Sokagakkai, you should support your boss, follow his directions and fulfill your responsibilities at work. This is the practice of true Buddhism. You must absolutely never confuse your position at work with your position in the organization. It is slander to take advantage of faith.

Consideration

You should not be so narrow-minded as to sever your relations with non-members or hold them at a distance. It is only common sense and a matter of social understanding to have contacts with the world.

Human beings must be broad-minded. For example, you should be open enough to feel you somehow want to help or encourage the people you know, even if they aren't members. Otherwise, you cannot be called a leader.

You have no way of knowing what role these

people will play in contributing to Kosen-rufu in the future. Kosen-rufu means enabling every person to make the most of himself. Leaders need such broad, human understanding.

Chapter Six: Womanhood

A woman's beauty

Faith enables a woman of any age to develop her own unique character and acquire grace. In our day, health, inner nobility and wisdom will become the standards of feminine beauty. I think a woman's outward appearance enhances these qualities. Having hope and self-confidence is important, but you must not become merely vain or arrogant.

Try to budget your personal expenses. You must be aware of your finances in order to plan your daily life effectively. Still, economy and stinginess are two different things.

A woman must be able to spare the effort to keep her hair neat and be well groomed.

Following the Gakkai

To follow the Gakkai means to worship the Gohonzon and practice earnestly for your own happiness and for others *(Jigyo Keta)*, as your individual circumstances permit. Practice Buddhism as though it were your favorite hobby. People who regard their practice as an obligation will impede the growth of our organization.

First of all, you must do a precise Gongyo every day, morning and evening. If you work, earn your salary by doing the best job possible. Become the kind of employee who makes others say, "What a wonderful girl." In Gakkai activities, receive guidance from your senior leaders. If you yourself are a leader, you have the responsibility to take good care of your members. Fulfilling all this constitutes following the Gakkai. You need not chase illusions or lose yourself in wild fantasies.

Our greatest memory

What are the most precious memories of your life? Memories of raising your children will be dear to you. Love, too, may bring pleasant recollections. Success in business is very satisfying to think back on. One accumulates all kinds of memories in the course of a lifetime.

But no matter how much wealth you've amassed, you can't hang on to it when you die. Romantic or sentimental memories will burst like bubbles. Dwelling on the past won't create any fortune; it's merely an idle amusement.

A woman's way of life

A woman should strive to become happy and fortunate, rather than great. I feel sorry for women who overreach themselves, impatient to become famous commentators or entertainers.

Depending upon your individual ability and education, you may achieve greatness as a result of your efforts for Kosen-rufu, based on your faith. That's fine, but you needn't make it your goal in life.

Leadership in the Sokagakkai is fundamentally different from leadership in society. From the standpoint of Buddhism, the highest honor is to fulfill a position of responsibility in the organization. Once, during an outdoor training session of the Suikokai,[1] a young man declared, "Someday I want to return to my home with honor." President Toda encouraged him, saying, "Aren't you a leader of the Sokagakkai? Isn't that the greatest possible honor?"

A woman should put vanity aside and consider carefully what road she should follow as a woman.

Flower arrangement

It's a mistake to think you can't create a pleasing flower arrangement because you can't afford expensive flowers. Spending a lot of money on flowers is an extravagant hobby. The soul of flower arrangement lies in doing it well, even if you don't spend much money.

---

[1] Suikokai—see footnote on page 104.

An old saying goes, "There is stillness in movement." In the midst of our hectic activities, it's good to have a few moments of quiet. Flower arrangement is not frivolity. It is meant to enrich a home and lend charm to our daily lives.

Wealth

Everything in the universe is transient *(Shogyo Mujo)*. Even material objects eventually vanish. The important thing is your fortune. Embracing the Gohonzon is the greatest wealth, as it is the source of gaining fortune. All other pleasures we enjoy are transient, because they belong to the worlds of *rapture* or Bodhisattva, not the world of *enlightenment.*

There is nothing awesome about millionaires. A true millionaire is one who has embraced the Gohonzon. It's as though he'd found Aladdin's lamp. The Lotus Sutra reads, "We have found a priceless gem without seeking it."

Marriage

The most important thing in marriage is your determination to continue your faith throughout life and never leave the Gohonzon.

Another person cannot bring you happiness. It's something you have to build yourself, through faith. Choosing a marriage partner is solely your own responsibility. It's important to consult your leaders and ask older people for their opinions, but ultimately, it is your decision.

※

Whether or not you choose a Sokagakkai member is entirely up to you. It's not something others should interfere with. If your faith is strong, eventually you can move your husband to practice and become a great person. Many women intend to maintain a strong practice after marrying, but instead their faith collapses and they suffer. In the end, I think an ideal marriage is one where both husband and wife share the same goals.

※

A woman won't necessarily be happy just because she marries young. Don't ever be in a rush to find a husband. Many people have established happy families even though they married late in life. Happiness does not depend on your age or on when you get married. It depends on your fortune.

While you're young, resolve to practice five or ten years to develop yourself and secure your eternal happiness. The ultimate victor is the one who perseveres in her practice, turning her individual circumstances into a springboard for growth.

You should think of your youth primarily as the time to practice, in order to build a foundation for lifelong happiness. Only your Gakkai activities will enable you to accumulate fortune, change your destiny and establish a happy marriage without fail. It's admirable to devote your youth to Kosen-rufu, without being caught up in trivial problems or swayed by circumstances. This is the road to your own human revolution.

Talk to your leaders often, about anything. Just because you belong to the young women's division, don't feel you have to settle your problems through the guidance of your young women's division leaders alone. It's a good idea to also consult your chapter, community and women's division leaders. Never try to show off or be obstinate.

Whether you marry or have children, no matter how much your circumstances may change, you should maintain an unwavering faith throughout your life.

The family

When a husband can't do Gakkai activities because of his commitments at work, his wife should practice that much harder. You can't solve this problem just by worrying about it. If it makes you anxious, chant Daimoku sincerely to change your situation and strive to improve your family.

Instead of worrying because your children don't chant, put your effort toward taking care of your members. Practice with the confidence that "I'll definitely convince my whole family to chant." Once you set a goal and strive for it, benefit will emerge inconspicuously.

The *Gosho* states, *One's Ichinen penetrates the entire universe.* This is the mysterious workings of a determined mind. *Ichinen* is an amazing thing. If you have this underlying *Ichinen*, sooner or later, you can influence your whole family to practice.

Sickness

Society carries on all kinds of activities and affairs for business reasons, and people form many relationships out of self-interest alone. Only the Sokagakkai is working solely for the happiness of others. In many cases, even hospitals are profit-oriented. Hospitals were originally supposed to embody a spirit of mercy, but sometimes they're extremely cruel, don't you think? In the end, the only way for people to live happily is through faith.

When someone gets sick, you should never say he has weak faith or that something is wrong with his practice. The Daishonin states, *One suffers from illness in the course of effacing bad karma.* Anyone may get sick while changing his destiny or erasing his previous misdeeds *(Zaisho Shometsu)*. You should give sick people your warmest encouragement.

Buddhism expounds the law of *Shiki Shin Funi*. As you practice, you will definitely become healthy in both body and mind. Over the long course of life, however, it's only natural that one grows old and deteriorates physically when he over-exerts himself. Firmly encourage anyone in this condition.

Seven kinds of wives

A Hinayana sutra reads, "There are seven kinds of wives in this world. The first is like a mother, the second like a younger sister, the third is a good friend, the fourth is a mate, the fifth is like a servant, the sixth is always jealous and the seventh is like a vampire who drains her husband's vitality."

The motherly wife, the sisterly wife, the wife who's a friend, the wife who warmly supports her husband and the wife like a devoted servant all have good qualities. The last two are like demons or wives who kill their husbands. They should be feared.

A woman who stops her husband from going to a discussion meeting is like an evil demon. A wife should not do wrong or betray her husband, or she will make him fail, even if he has great potential. Such a wife is terrible. On the other hand, a woman who encourages her husband becomes a good friend, or *Zenchishiki*, to him.

People's opinions

A child is overweight, so the doctor tells the mother, "He may die young," and naturally she agonizes over it. Such a doctor is totally without mercy. Then, when asked if he could help the boy, he replies, "It's nothing too unusual." What a glaring contradiction!

No one can foresee what will happen tomorrow, much less the future of a child. The Gohonzon is the only thing you can rely on. It's important to listen to other people's opinions, evaluating them from the standpoint of faith. But you must not be completely swayed by them.

Worries

Everyone has worries. Troubles are part of living, and you can never free yourself from them entirely. What counts is the ability to view your problems objectively. This you can only achieve through faith. Worrying alone will not help anyone, but when your problems make you chant Daimoku to the Gohonzon and strengthen your faith, you will start changing your destiny.

This is the principle of changing problems into *enlightenment.*

Greatest joy

No matter how smart you are, you'll lose out if you're not bright and cheerful. This is the key to faith. Nichiren Daishonin said, *Nam-myoho-renge-kyo is the joy of joys. Joys* means your own happiness; *the joy of joys* is the experience of enabling others to become happy.

Sincerity

Sokagakkai leaders should fulfill their social obligations graciously and be courteous. I think this is not mere formality but a sincere and truly humanistic attitude. Ignoring common sense contradicts faith.

Entering college

Some people benefit from going to college while others with no higher education succeed in the family business. Still others lose their health by studying too hard. So long as you're undecided, there's no end to it. Make up your mind, decide your course and map out a plan in your chosen field.

Even Gakudo Ozaki[1] and Alfred Nobel supposedly suffered many setbacks in school. Failing once or twice in the entrance exams doesn't really decide your success or failure in life.

※

Grade school, the university and society itself each have their own standards of evaluation. Doing well in college doesn't necessarily mean you'll do well out in the world. You should advance determinedly with your faith as your foundation.

Children

As a parent, you will find it natural to worry about your children. It's your responsibility to raise them well, no matter how busy you are. A parent's love shows itself in this way. It's totally wrong to rationalize your child's poor behavior by saying you don't have time for him.

The senior leaders' children are all growing up splendidly. A child's sound development ultimately depends on the family itself. Look at yourself and strive to protect your family so you can raise fine children.

---

[1] Gakudo Ozaki (1859-1954)—statesman noted for defending democracy. He waged a battle through the press against policy of dissolving opposition parties.

A mother cherishes a deep heartfelt love for her children. When she faces the Gohonzon, that love is contained in all her Daimoku, even when she isn't specifically chanting for them. Although she may not always be consciously aware of it, her love protects them constantly.

Women

If you think of yourself as a tamer of wild beasts, then you can lead your husband, regardless of his personality. The *Gosho* states, *A woman follows her husband, but actually makes him follow her.*

As a wife, never act like a Gakkai leader at home. You should work diligently for your family's peace and happiness. At home, be a good wife and mother, and in Gakkai activities, be one who will fight for the sake of unhappy people.

A woman must be careful not to become the disciple of her child. A mother whose whole life is absorbed in her children often cannot maintain a strong practice. She can neither develop herself as a woman nor raise her children successfully. Her attitude will eventually affect her husband and make him ineffective at work. A mother must be the firm, staunch support of her family.

A woman who is a slave to her children is like the demon Kishimojin in the sutras. Ultimately she will destroy her child's independence and hinder his growth. Even her physical appearance will reflect the ugly nature of a woman who crushes her child's potential.

Whether or not your husband and children embrace the Gohonzon depends on their relationship with Buddhism from the past. However, Nichiren Daishonin taught that if even one person carries out a sincere practice, his whole family will receive benefit and eventually begin to chant.

It's important to constantly deepen your faith and broaden your understanding. You don't need to show off; it's pointless. Women's division members especially should be as fresh, bright and youthful as the young women's division. However, I hope you'll also be brave. If you look at those contemporary leaders who are most respected by others, they all have courage. They spontaneously go wherever they are needed. They are always ready to move. Faith, stated differently, is courage.

A man should draw vitality from the Gohonzon to win at his job or business, and carry out his human revolution with confidence. A woman too should have strong faith in order to encourage her husband and develop herself so her children won't have cause to make fun of her. She should become a good mother and a wise and gentle wife, and be respected by everyone. Her appearance should reflect the beauty of neatness and dignity.

"Frost and dewdrops"

The Fugen sutra reads, "Bad karma is dispelled like frost or dewdrops in the sun." When you worship the Gohonzon, all your past misdeeds will be erased, just as sunlight evaporates dew or frost. One who can entrust everything to the Gohonzon and put his mind at rest will definitely become happy."

The chapter women's chief

A chapter women's chief is in a position to offer her opinions to the chapter and assistant chapter chief, and she should do so by all means. This has been a basic principle of our organization since it began. Former President Toda once said, "We must encourage the growth of sincere chapter women's chiefs; for one thing, to restrain the chapter and assistant chapter chiefs when they go to extremes." A chapter chief should respect the chapter women's leaders. He must never regard them as subordinates under his command.

Widows

Parental love for children borders on mercy, states a passage from the *Gosho*. But parental love still falls short of mercy. As Sokagakkai leaders, you are leaders of an organization based on mercy. On my behalf, you should raise your juniors warmly and respect sincere individuals from the bottom of your hearts. It's important to make this your first priority. A leader must be someone who is progressing, is honest, has a seeking mind for Buddhism and who also has high spirits. Whether the members become happy or not depends solely on their leader. I want you to pass on this principle to your juniors as a tradition for the future.

Please be especially warm when encouraging a widow. Become closer to her than a sister, basing your relationship on faith. Never look down on her. Buddhism is the world of mercy, which enables even the most miserable person to find happiness. You will never understand the brave struggles and sorrows of a widow if you haven't lost your own husband. The Daishonin's mercy is infinitely deeper than the love parents have for their children. As his disciples, we, the leaders, must be considerate.

Faith should not be emotional. The Gohonzon is your ultimate master, because it possesses the three virtues of sovereign, teacher and parent. Stand up. Be strong. Love and respect the Gohonzon as though you'd found your eternal husband.

Many women will become widows someday. In a sense, they practice now so that they won't be crushed by their loss when that time comes. As a widow, you must be able to calmly encourage them to follow your example.

Encouraging widows

When your own worries trouble you and make you chant, you're progressing. This is called "the valiant and untiring practice," or *Yumyo Shojin.* Even so, you should be bold enough to set out on new ventures.

Contemporary politicians have no "valiant untiring practice" to develop themselves. They cling to wealth and power, and their fortune vanishes. Gakkai members can make phenomenal progress through their practice of *Yumyo Shojin.* It's fine to have confidence bordering on audacity. If you're swayed by the trends of society, you'll be unhappy. Advance with strong faith as your foundation.

~~~

Even if you lose your husband, you should think of the Gohonzon as your husband. I hope you will follow the right path throughout your life, burning with hope.

Never demean yourself. Live the kind of life that even women with husbands will envy. Because you must raise your children alone and struggle for Kosen-rufu without a husband, you will definitely receive immense benefit. Don't be afraid to hold high hopes. The Daishonin wrote many letters to encourage widows. You should read the *Gosho* as your guide for living.

Personal circumstances

A woman should always be youthful. It's your own loss if you're not. It's a defeat to be noticeably haggard from quarreling with your husband, caring for your children or other demands of daily life.

The women's division of the Sokagakkai is a gathering of sharp, confident and youthful leaders who can write and speak with conviction. This women's division, without parallel in the world, is realizing the lasting liberation of women. No other women's organization can surpass ours.

Many kinds of women are needed for Kosen-rufu. Some can fight like Sennichi-ama who served the Daishonin personally. Others are more like Shijo Kingo's wife, who supported her husband at the front line of the campaign by quietly exerting her full effort behind the scenes. Still others have a mission like the widow Nichigen-ama, who devoted her whole life to Buddhism. Develop your full potential as a leader within your own circumstances.

Foundation of Kosen-rufu

Those who embrace the Gohonzon are the foundation of Kosen-rufu, regardless of the role they play. If you worship the Gohonzon you'll gain benefit regardless of your position. Don't downgrade yourself just because you're not a leader.

Some people are best suited to be active as

group or district leaders, while others can better utilize their talents as senior leaders, guiding the members. You must consider each person individually.

For instance, you may need to think seriously whether you should promote a district leader to chapter women's chief, or if it's better to let her continue activities in her present position.

There is some validity in making someone a leader because of her success in Shakubuku or because she's bright-spirited, but this isn't everything you should consider.

Former President Toda resigned as general director to become an ordinary member. However, he himself did not change in the least.

You can tell if a leader is great when her position changes. She must become someone who is loved and trusted, regardless of the role she takes. If she becomes conceited because she's appointed a leader, her juniors will gradually overtake her.

Ideal women

It's ideal for women's division leaders to be

loved and trusted by the members, because the members of the Sokagakkai are actually all Buddhas and Bodhisattvas of the universe.

A woman should never hate others, envy them their happiness or hinder their growth. Such an attitude runs counter to faith and will defeat you later on. Hold your own course straight.

Women leaders should have an air of dignity and neatness.

A modern woman can't be frail or helpless. You need robust vitality. If you develop your capabilities while young, you can stand firm no matter what happens in the long course of your life.

It's terrible when women compete selfishly to promote their own husbands or children. There is definitely no place for this in our organization.

Live fully till your last moment, no matter what. At a crucial moment, women too must have the courage to protect the Gohonzon and the Sokagakkai, without retreating a single step.

Chapter Seven: Culture

Civilization

Christianity was one of the pillars of Western civilization, and materialism has given rise to the prosperity of civilization today. The Sokagakkai does not oppose these doctrines but encompasses them and gives them direction. Buddhism is a much broader philosophy, commanding a total view of the universe.

The doctrine and practice of our organization is to develop great educators, scientists, artists, businessmen and workers and to encourage research in every field of scholastic and scientific inquiry, based on the Daishonin's life-philosophy. Capable men will emerge through this practice just as plants and trees grow in soil. This is how Kosen-rufu will come about.

We can never achieve worldwide Kosen-rufu unless we become broad-minded enough to understand materialism, spiritualism or any other movement or philosophy. Right now we are advancing step by step, always taking the future into consideration. It's a serious misunderstanding to label the Sokagakkai as exclusive.

People and nations

One new philosophy can bring about the rise of a nation. When a nation flourishes, fortune follows, making all factors work for the people's prosperity.

All people want peace and freedom. Human desires are the same everywhere; the only difference lies in which philosophy they adopt as a means of fulfilling them.

There should be no war. Both the leaders and general public of every nation all share this same feeling. But people easily become arrogant because of personal feelings or ambitions, and the life of *anger* or conflict comes to the fore.

Science and Buddhism

The question arises as to how Buddhism views scientific research. It's jumping the gun to immediately start quoting the *Gosho* on this point. Of course, all science does take on new significance when viewed from the absolute standpoint of Buddhist philosophy *(Zettaimyo)*. However, science follows an inductive approach while Buddhism is deductive. It's important to recognize the difference between these two methods. If you make faith the basis of your observation, you can naturally see the contradictions in science.

Whether he was teaching astronomy or law, former President Toda would first make his listeners grasp the subject exactly as the books described it. Then he would explain it in the light of Buddhism. Science in particular serves as a preface to Buddhism and should be given careful consideration from this standpoint.

Western philosophy and Buddhism

Former President Toda once said that Western philosophy is like a toy sword, which definitely applies, whether we're talking about Marxism, pragmatism, the philosophy of Kant, Hegel's dialectic, analytic philosophy, existentialism, phenomenology or any other system of thought. All are generally well organized and precise in their theoretical framework. However, they only sound impressive. They can neither help anyone achieve human revolution nor rid the world of suffering. When it comes down to fact, what have they actually accomplished?

The Daishonin's Buddhism, the core of Eastern thought, is a living philosophy backed up by practice and verified through actual proof in daily life. It is a true sword, whose keen edge can cut through the worries and sorrows of both the individual and society.

Soka University

I am firmly determined to establish Soka University. Today's educational world cannot possibly develop men with the capabilities needed to complete Kosen-rufu. This university must be established at all cost, and I intend to do so, incorporating the spirit of first President Makiguchi and the guidance of former President Toda.

The entrance exams will be like those of any other university. They should by no means be unusually difficult or be easier for Gakkai members. Yet on second thought, they may have to be even tougher than Tokyo University's exams. It's not hard to guess why, if you imagine the growth of our elementary, junior high and senior high school division members in five or seven years' time.

Economics

Politics decide the life or death of a nation, and politics are backed up by economics. For this reason, economics are vitally important and should be based on a sound philosophy. Inasmuch as we possess the supreme philosophy, we can become economists capable of grasping the true picture of our changing economy, which contemporary economists have thus far been unable to do.

Chant Daimoku, study hard and become a great economist. Halfway efforts won't get you anywhere. Resolve to create a new and vital economic system.

Clear thinking

Few people can boast of a good memory. Memorizing is a matter of effort. When you chant Daimoku and work hard at it, everything you try to remember will become part of you. That is your human revolution.

People fall roughly into one of two categories: men of fortune and men of wisdom. According to the Daishonin's teachings, both wisdom and fortune well up from our lives when we chant Daimoku. Nam-myoho-renge-kyo contains both fortune and wisdom. You yourself are a small universe, so when you chant Daimoku to the Gohonzon, all the treasures and vast wisdom of the universe will appear in your own life.

※※※

When you gauge yourself according to the depth of the supreme life-philosophy and the swift pace and scope of our organization, you may feel you are falling behind. The determination you make at that moment to grow and keep up with the organization will accelerate your human revolution and change of destiny.

※※※

Have confidence in yourself. You can't develop your faith when you're apple-polishing or acting emotionally. Rest assured that regardless of your circumstances or role in society, you are leading the noblest life possible because you've embraced true Buddhism.

※※※

Former President Toda used to say, drawing a line, "Even if you're smart, what difference does it make if you fall above this line or below it? The winner is the one who persists in his efforts." A well-known saying goes, "Genius is effort," so why not work and study as hard as you can?

༄༅

Today's critics and scholars are convinced of their own brilliance, but often it amounts to no more than mere techniques of theory. Their skills are in no way superior to the skills of shoemaking or farming. Sokagakkai leaders may even study more widely than they do. Don't make the mistake of thinking scholars are a special breed of men. It's an illusion. We cannot achieve a religious or cultural revolution with such attitudes.

༄༅

Some shoemakers are men of remarkable genius, and some clerks have fine memories and excellent judgment. This is good. You should all become top people in your own fields.

The Third Civilization

The Third Civilization, a humanistic society and Kosen-rufu are all the same thing. The word

"Kosen-rufu" means the will of the Daishonin. From the standpoint of culture or civilization, it indicates the Third Civilization. From the standpoint of politics and sociology, Kosen-rufu refers to a humanistic society. By way of analogy, sometimes a man is called by name and at other times by his title or position. Some people say "the True Buddha" and others say "Nichiren Daishonin."

The music of the Third Civilization

The rise of a single philosophy will bring about a whole new culture. Great art and music accompanied the spread of Christianity. New trends in music and science are also emerging in the communist world. Kosen-rufu, the spread of the Daishonin's Buddhism, will give rise to new values based on this philosophy. When that happens, the music of the Third Civilization will be heard.

Don't expect a unique musical style to appear. Rather, you, yourself, should practice, keep pace with the progress of the Sokagakkai and develop your capabilities to suit the times. When you create music with that *Ichinen*, that in itself is the music of the Third Civilization.

Writing

Very few people have confidence in their writing. Everyone has these doubts, but don't stop trying. Study and work hard to keep a step ahead of others. Your efforts will determine whether or not you achieve greatness.

Leo Tolstoy is said to have rewritten each sentence time after time, aware that his works would remain for posterity. Although a literary giant, he still made painstaking efforts.

Goethe once remarked, "One cannot say what he wishes because he tries to speak in high-flown language." If you say exactly what you feel, you should have no trouble.

It's not hard to write exactly as you feel. Some people find writing a chore because they write out of falseness or vanity, or in order to sound impressive.

Eiji Yoshikawa's[1] style is completely different from Jun'ichiro Tanizaki's.[2] Today's authors

---

[1] Eiji Yoshikawa (1892-1964)—popular novelist known for his modern retelling of *Romance of the Three Kingdoms* and his tale of the great swordsman, *Miyamoto Musashi*.

[2] Jun'ichiro Tanizaki (1886-1965)—famous novelist. Many works are now translated into English. Known for great rendering of ancient *Tale of Genji* to modern Japanese.

each have their individual manner of expression. Everyone should write in his own style.

Theses

A thesis must always be logical. It should not be a statement of personal beliefs. You need to establish a logical framework and develop the subject. In the conclusion, you can draw from practical experience or clearly summarize.

One possible format consists of an introduction, main body and application. Another approach involves a general discussion, followed by a detailed analysis and conclusion. The key points of your thesis must be clear to any reader.

***

The sutra is a speech. Sakyamuni's teachings and Nichiren Daishonin's *Gosho* are ultimate examples of the war of words. Through doing Shakubuku, we acquire a correct viewpoint, master the ability to convince people and develop a fine verbal strategy.

***

You should develop yourself through writing. Become a writer whose name alone will make readers say, "If it's his work, I've got to read it!" Truly powerful sentences are crafted through experience.

The voice

The *Gosho* states, *One's voice expresses his thoughts; therefore, his mind takes shape through his voice. His thoughts represent the law of mind* (Shinpo) *and his voice, the law of matter* (Shiki-ho). *The voice* (Shiki) *comes from the mind* (Shin).

The voice is alive. Some people can touch the hearts of others when they speak, not through the literal meaning of their words, but through the broad experience and understanding which their voices convey.

Naturally, any speech should make a point. Speech is called *Kegi,* because it is expressed through a formal system of words. Through a person's speech, you can discern the thoughts and beliefs underlying his words. These thoughts are called *Keho.* Guidance must never become formality or a mere stringing together of words. It should pierce people's hearts.

Capability

"Keep a sword in your mouth and a dagger in your hand," goes an old saying. "A sword in your mouth" means eloquence and the mastery of languages. "A dagger in your hand" is the war of words and ideas. The sword and the dagger symbolize discussion, which will supplant weapons, authority and financial power.

Many students today seem solely concerned with getting their diplomas and finding good jobs. What society needs, however, is not more diplomas but capable people. Completing formalities, such as receiving your diploma, is *Shakumon.* What you're actually capable of doing is *Honmon.* Capability is the watchword of the Sokagakkai.

Our critics

No one is more selfish than contemporary leaders. We ourselves are sincerely carrying out the faith, practice and study of Nichiren Daishonin's Buddhism night and day for the sake of the people. Are those who criticize us open enough to even try to understand Buddhism? They are imprisoned by their own conceit.

How much have politicians and critics helped the people? They only exploit them and take their money. Isn't that how they earn a living?

We do not make our living from our religion. We don't need their praise. As the *Gosho* states, *To be praised by a fool is the greatest shame.* You should be able to see through them well enough to know that they only criticize us for their own advantage, or to earn a living.

Uncrowned kings

"I am a man of the common people with neither wealth nor power. Yet in the public eye, I am an uncrowned king. I am a hero of the press." One who fights with this conviction, courage and hope can truly be called a king without a crown.

We too have neither titles nor fame, but we are kings in the world of religion. You should advance with this understanding.

Expression

It is possible to look serious while laughing inwardly. Some people may seem to be listening to you sincerely while mocking you in their hearts. As a leader, keep your ear to the ground.

The important thing is not someone's facial expression but whether or not he wholeheartedly trusts you. You must never act arrogantly or put on airs.

You cannot move others unless you yourself are moved. This is an expression of *Esho Funi* and the motion of life itself. Without real warmth, passion and concern, you cannot move anyone.

Criticism and practice

Criticizing others is easy. That's why weak people love to criticize. Strong people love to practice. Youth should be men of practice rather than critics. Become men who can stand on behalf of justice and smile amid storms of criticism.

Music and youth

Professional musicians aren't necessarily great. Truly great writers and musicians all struggled through hardships. Today's musicians are as shallow as the weekly magazines. This is why no great writers or musicians are emerging right now.

Someone once asked, "I want to be a musician, but my father insists I take over the family business. What shall I do?" The answer will become clear as his faith deepens. All men have hopes they cannot easily realize, which accounts for the different roads people take in life. Never despair or think you're a special case. Favorable circumstances don't necessarily produce great musicians. Muster your faith, hang on to your hopes, and whatever your circumstances, start from there and resolve to become a top musician. Doors will definitely open up for you. If you continue your practice, you'll be able to express your talent and enjoy life thoroughly, regardless of the course you decide to pursue. You should be confident of this and step forward with assurance.

A nation without songs will be ruined. Where people sing, the country flourishes.

People without interests are colorless. No one follows them, because they hold no attraction. It's important to have at least one specific interest and strive to deepen your general knowledge and understanding.

Self

Always be yourself. A man tends to seem important when he stands in front of a large group of people or appears on stage. When you become a leader, people listen to you. It's easy to fall under the illusion that all of a sudden you're great or wonderful. You should become a truly capable leader who will not be blinded by his own position.

A car with a tiny engine can't move against a strong wind, but if the engine's powerful, it doesn't matter how hard the wind blows. "Prepare now and avoid trouble later" and "care prevents accidents" are common sayings. If a small engine won't serve your purposes, get yourself a bigger one. When demons threaten to overcome you, strongly summon up your faith.

The afterglow of success in a culture festival is like an aurora. The colors of an aurora shift moment by moment, and people's minds change just as rapidly. Today's deep emotion will fade as time passes. Never be intoxicated by momentary success or relax in your efforts.

In bar gymnastics, many people can skillfully perform in unison with the help of the same bar. Faith is the same way. If you stay close to the bar and hang on tightly, you won't go wrong. This is called *Itai Doshin.*

The public

You cannot move others if you yourself are not moved. Your writing comes to life when something touches you deeply and you write it down to the best of your ability. An article written merely to meet a deadline cannot reach people's hearts.

Don't be taken in by the words "the public." You're one of the public too. What you write from your own heart will move others. This is *Ichinen Sanzen* in action. Egoism has no place here. When you write with the public in mind and communicate your joy, you will naturally elicit a great response.

Don't force your personal opinions on other people. Your family and your co-workers are both smaller versions of the general public, so there's no excuse for not knowing public opinion.

Mass media

The press should represent the nation and guide the people. It's irresponsible to play up to the public by printing only criticism or establishing a policy of, say, seventy per cent eulogizing and thirty per cent censure. Journalism should take a fair and penetrating view, rising above selfish interests.

Reader contributions sometimes reflect the views of the public at large, but at other times you should regard them strictly as offbeat opinions and not be influenced by them. Learning to make this distinction is part of a leader's training.

At one time I edited a children's magazine. I tried to find out which sections the children generally read, and I discovered they all liked the comics. At first I thought we should include more comics, but on the other hand, the parents might not approve. I debated endlessly over how to apportion the copy.

The time to fight

Faith is a constant struggle with the demon *Dairokuten-no Mao,* and in faith, we should fight without compromise. In practical affairs, however, it's foolish to needlessly confront a powerful enemy. You should use good judgment. When you see that defeat is inevitable, the sensible thing to do is retreat and wait for the right moment to begin the next round.

Tokugawa Ieyasu[1] fled from his enemies but returned later to win a great victory. He understood the strategic principle of waiting for the right time. One who does nothing but retreat is a coward. Knowing when to fight and when to retreat takes a wise man.

Reading

Some people enjoy reading but read only for the sake of knowledge, failing to absorb the material and make it a part of their lives. Others don't like to read. However, the Daishonin taught us, *Exert yourself in the two ways of practice and study.* Make a serious effort to read so that you can advance one more step in your human revolution.

---

[1] Tokugawa Ieyasu—see footnote on page 114.

When you read a book again, years later, you will find it more meaningful. One approach to reading is to make a resolution to read so many books per month. Read the *Gosho* as your foundation. Not only will you gradually come to understand it, but you can read other books in the light of the *Gosho's* teachings.

In the future, many young people may become diplomats or play leading roles in international affairs. Others may travel throughout the world as leaders of the Sokagakkai. If they lack knowledge and experience, they will find themselves in an awkward situation.

Reading methods

I began to make notes on my reading after the war ended, right around the time I met former President Toda. I would underline certain parts and jot down passages that struck me, because writing them down fixed them in my mind. I still have those notebooks. You should read in your own way and not worry about the formality of a particular method.

As a youth, Stalin devoured Victor Hugo's *Quatre-vingt-treize,* which was banned in Russia at the time. Mao Tse-tung read the *Romance of the Three Kingdoms* and the *Tales of Suiko,*[1] among others. Former President Toda's favorites were all stories about revolution, such as *Quatre-vingt-treize, The Eternal City, Yui Shosetsu,* the *Tales of Suiko* and *Chinzei Yumiharizuki.*

Historical perspective

All history reveals the true aspect of life *(Shoho Jisso).* The whole of contemporary society is a miniature of history. I have little confidence in past accounts. Newspapers and magazines don't even report accurately about events that happened in the last ten or fifteen years. You can see this when you read distorted accounts of the Sokagakkai. When you read history that dates back one or two thousand years, you should bear this in mind.

---

[1]*Romance of the Three Kingdoms* and the *Tales of Suiko* are both Chinese classics. *Suiko* recounts the adventures of a group of chivalrous bandits—actually exiles from a corrupt, bloodthirsty government—who unite to aid oppressed people. Hall Cain's *Eternal City* describes the heroism of two modern Italian revolutionaries. *Yui Shosetsu* is the story of a brilliant strategist who led an unsuccessful revolt against the Tokugawa government. *Chinzei Yumiharizuki* describes the samurai ethic.

True history is right now. The question in viewing history is whether or not you can interpret it correctly, which depends on your historical perspective. Our view of history is based on our faith.

The ten worlds

Any novel falls within the realm of the *ten worlds*. Today's novels seldom go beyond the worlds of *hell, hunger, animality* and *anger*. When one embraces the Gohonzon and brings out the condition of *enlightenment* within his own life, he can create healthy literature and art.

When I read Hugo's *Quatre-vingt-treize* with former President Toda, he would point out, "This part shows the world of *animality*. This one expresses *tranquility*. This one, *anger*. And this part shows the actions of Bodhisattva. . ."

The same holds true with music. There is great music which evokes the world of Bodhisattva and cheap music which calls forth that of *anger*. The doleful invocations of Nembutsu express the world of *hell*.

Study

Youth must tirelessly absorb knowledge, grow and experience new worlds. Daimoku and the practice and study of true Buddhism are the bases of your development. You are not really youth without the drive to master something.

First President Makiguchi said, "When you stop advancing, you are no longer young."

Second President Toda said, "One who carries his youthful convictions and passion throughout life is the greatest of men. Fame and wealth count for nothing."

What I wish to say is, "Youth is construction." Those who burn with the passion to build are truly young.

Glossary

BODHISATTVA — One devoted to practicing the Daishonin's Buddhism for his own *enlightenment* and for others' happiness. Also see *ten worlds*.

BON'NO SOKU BODAI — Transforming earthly desires or problems *(Bon'no)* into *enlightenment (Bodai)* by practicing Buddhism.

DAIROKUTEN-NO MAO — Strongest obstacle in the way of one's *enlightenment*.

ESHO FUNI — Inseparability of man and his environment. One's surroundings mirror his own life-condition, and he in turn is influenced by his surroundings.

HA-WAGOSO — Disrupting the unity of Sokagakkai members.

HENDOKU IYAKU — Means "changing poison into medicine." Transforming problems or obstacles into fortune and happiness through practicing Buddhism.

HONMATSU KUKYO-TO — Consistency from beginning to end. When one is mentally experiencing *hell*, his appearance, thoughts, surroundings, relations, actions, results, etc. will all mirror the condition of *hell*.

HONMON — Absolute or supreme teachings, as opposed to transient teachings *(Shakumon)*. Latter half of Sakyamuni's Lotus Sutra which expounds the eternity of life and the nature of *enlightenment*; also means the Daishonin's Buddhism as compared to Sakyamuni's. More broadly, *Honmon* refers to practice, as opposed to theory.

HON'IN-MYO — The highest cause, meaning that anyone can develop, regardless of his destiny or past causes, when he resolves to practice true Buddhism. Also means the spirit of fresh determination or "start now."

HOSSHAKU KEMPON — Breaking through into a new dimension or higher stage of life through intense effort and practice.

ICHINEN — The totality of one's life in the present moment. Having a strong *Ichinen* toward something means that one's entire being, far beyond the conscious levels of existence, is focused on that objective.

ICHINEN SANZEN — 3,000 worlds in a momentary state of existence. Fundamental

Buddhist theory clarifying nature of life. Revealed in the Lotus Sutra, systematized by T'ien-t'ai and materialized in the Gohonzon by Nichiren Daishonin

ICHINEN ZUIKI — Profound joy of being alive in the present moment, arising from one's life as a result of faith.

INGA GUJI — Simultaneous nature of cause and effect. Superficially, there appears to be a gap in time between a cause and its effect, but in reality, the effect exists in the same moment that the cause is made.

ISSHO JOBUTSU — Attaining *enlightenment* in this lifetime, or lifetime practice for *enlightenment*.

ITAI DOSHIN — Different bodies, one mind, or unity based on faith. The many different types of people in the Sokagakkai are all bound together by the common goal of Kosen-rufu.

JAKKO-DO — The pure land of Buddha. Viewed in earlier teachings as a remote, ideal realm, today *Jakko-do* is any place the Gohonzon is enshrined.

JIDO BOMPU — Appearing as an ordinary person. Nichiren Daishonin appeared ordinary to prove that anyone could attain *enlightenment*.

JIGYO KETA — Practice for one's own sake and for others'.

JIHI — Buddhist mercy. Literally, to remove suffering and give happiness.

JIYU-NO BOSATSU — Bodhisattvas of the Earth. Promised in the Lotus Sutra to spread Nam-myoho-renge-kyo in Mappo. Anyone who practices Nichiren Daishonin's Buddhism.

JO RAKU GA JO — Four virtues of eternity, happiness, true identity and purity; manifested through chanting Nam-myoho-renge-kyo.

KEGI — Means formality, while KEHO means the law or fundamental meaning underlying it.

KYOCHI MYOGO — Fusion of the objective world *(Kyo)* and oneself *(chi)*. Fundamentally, the supreme happiness or Buddhahood experienced in fusing one's life *(chi)* with the Gohonzon *(Kyo)*. Also any harmonious dynamic fusion between oneself and the environment; e.g. a businessman and his work.

LOTUS SUTRA — Sakyamuni's highest teaching, which revealed the eternity of life and the nature of *enlightenment*. Also, the highest Buddhist teaching in any given period. In Shoho, Sakyamuni's sutra of the same name; in Zoho, T'ien-t'ai's *Maka Shikan,* and in Mappo, Nam-myoho-renge-kyo or the Gohonzon of the Three Great Secret Laws.

MA — Devils, or one's own destructive nature, which emerges to hinder his practice.

MAIJI SA ZE NEN — "I always have this in mind." The Buddha is always concerned with how to lead people to *enlightenment.*

MAKA SHIKAN — Book of Great Enlightenment, taught by T'ien-t'ai in 594. Supreme teaching of the Zoho period; theoretical explanation of *Ichinen Sanzen.*

MYOKAKU — Ultimate *enlightenment.* In Sakyamuni's Buddhism, one went through a series of fifty-two stages to reach a form of *enlightenment* called *Tokaku,* which is still incomplete. Only from there could he proceed to *Myokaku.* In the Daishonin's Buddhism, one attains *Myokaku* directly.

NINPO IKKA — Oneness of person and Law. The life of Nichiren Daishonin and the Law of Nam-myoho-renge-kyo are one. The Gohonzon is the perfect entity of *Ninpo Ikka.* In daily life, person is oneself, and Law, the goal to which he aspires.

NINPO SHORETSU — Inconsistency of person and Law. Failure to live up to one's stated beliefs.

ROKUDO RINNE — The cycle of *hell, hunger, animality, anger, tranquility* and *rapture.* Being trapped in a continuous repetition of these lower worlds.

SANRUI - NO GOTEKI — *Three strong enemies.* Friends or relatives, other religious organizations, and government leaders, journalists or other powerful individuals who oppose true Buddhism.

SANSHO SHIMA — "Three obstacles and four devils" which hinder one's practice.

SHAKUMON — Transient teachings. First half of Sakyamuni's Lotus Sutra, or when compared to the Daishonin's teachings, all of Sakyamuni's Buddhism. *Shakumon* also means theory as opposed to practice. See *Honmon.*

SHIKI SHIN FUNI — Inseparability of body and mind, or matter and energy. Encompasses the two major philosophical streams of materialism and spiritualism. Ultimate principle of the Daishonin's life-philosohy.

SHITEI FUNI — Oneness of master and disciple, or the master-disciple relationship as taught in Buddhism. The prime point of Buddhism.

SHOGYO MUJO — The concept that all phenomena in the universe are transient.

SHO RYO BYO SHI — The four sufferings of birth, aging, sickness and death.

SHOTEN ZENJIN —Buddhist gods. Natural functions of the universe which appear in many different forms to protect those who practice true Buddhism.

SHUJO SHO YURAKU — "The place where people enjoy their lives." This world. When one practices he can enjoy life under any circumstances.

TATSUNOKUCHI PERSECUTION — Unsuccessful attempt by the government to execute the Daishonin. Escaping death, he fulfilled the predictions of the Lotus Sutra and proved himself the True Buddha.

TEN WORLDS — Basic life-conditions which everyone experiences from one moment to another. They are: *hell, hunger, animality, anger, tranquility, rapture, learning, absorption, aspiration for enlightenment* and *enlightenment*.

THIRD CIVILIZATION — Humanistic society based on the Gohonzon, harmonizing the two philosophical mainstreams of materialism and spiritualism.

THREE EVIL PATHS — *Hell, hunger* and *animality*.

TOKAKU — See *Myokaku*.

YUMYO SHOJIN — "Valiant and untiring practice." One's ceaseless efforts to develop himself and make others happy through the Buddhist practice.

ZENCHISHIKI —Good friend in Buddhism; one who spurs another on to practice harder.

ZETTAIMYO —Viewing ideas or phenomena from the absolute standpoint of Buddhist teachings, opposite of *Sotaimyo*, or comparing Buddhism with other ideologies.

ZOHO — Second thousand-year period following Sakyamuni's death, in which Buddhism declined and became formalized.

ZUIEN SHINNYO-NO CHI — Exercising good judgment or wisdom according to the circumstances.

ZUIHO BINI — Strictly fulfilling the basic practice of Buddhism yet adapting its formalities to local custom and tradition.

ZUIJII — Basing one's actions on the absolute standard of Buddhist teachings. Opposite of *Zuitai*, or basing one's actions on the thoughts, feelings, reactions, etc. of others.

Index

accomplishment, 73; a measure of human worth, 188; in past, 79, 164

action, 172; consistency of, 168

activities, 101; and study, 170; consistent, 172; spirit of, 77; voluntary, 172; work and, 166

adaptability, 60, 61, 120, 135

advancement, 79, 95, 275; of faith, 83, 89, 99, 146, 156; through Daimoku, 83; Kosen-rufu, 92; with fresh determination, 215

adversity, 161; also see hardships; obstacles

affection, 73

age, 188; for marriage, 233

alertness, 257

appearance, physical, 96

arrogance, 56, 191, 223, 265 also see conceit

art, 274

aspect, true, 156

assistance, see support

atmosphere, of guidance, 109 of meetings, 61, 66, 109

attitude, determines environment, 99; of leaders, 48, 74, 94

authoritarianism, 33, 72, 97

awareness, 165

backsliding, 120, 215

beauty, of a woman, 229

Bodhisattva, of the Earth 91, 176; solitary, 131

Bon'no soku Bodai, 125, 206

broad-mindedness, 13, 225, 253

Buddha, defined, 107

Buddhist gods, 138, 218

budgeting, 229; also see finances, money

business, 223

campaigns, direction of 172; *Ichinen* during, 202

capable men, 15, 24, 102, 126, 209, 217, 263; development as, 76, 211; emergence of, 24, 26, 31; raising of, 253

carelessness, 121, 131, 133

cause and effect, perception of, 167; simultaneity of 103, 108, 167, 174, 184

change, of mind, 149; also see adaptability

character, of leaders, 26, 92; of youth 74; strength of 200, 208

cheerfulness, 116, 179, 239; in Shakubuku, 92, 125

children, 240

clarity, need for, 56

closeness, to leaders, 59

commitment, to practice, 169

common sense, 239; in ac-

tivities, 170, 174, 202; with members, 82
communication, among leaders, 129; person-to-person, 65
compassion, 89
composure, 56, 123, 208
concern, for one's members 55, 97; for parents, 194
conceit, 32, 44, 57, 131, 154, 168, 191; also see arrogance
concreteness, of guidance, 52, 61
conduct, of leaders, 95
confidence, 34, 95, 170, 206; depends on faith, 149; in face of obstacles, 26, 114, 201; instilling, 52; key to victory, 128; leaders', 208; of mission, 171; self-, 14, 65, 246, 258; also see conviction
consideration, 40, 54, 56, 58; for parents, 194
consistency, 77; beginning to end, 175; of daily struggle 164; of practice, 79, 168, 172, 205; of temperament, 162
conviction, 58, 82, 98, 153; in Shakubuku, 138; of Kosen-rufu, 39; also see confidence
courage, 14, 120, 123, 151, 245; capacity and wisdom, 126; unyielding faith, 103
courtesy, 223
creativity, 203, 231

criticism, 20, 21, 94, 149, 180, 181, 266; by leaders 16; of the Sokagakkai, 58, 208, 264
crucial moments, 84
culture, 266, 268

daily life, faith in, 106, 168, 174; struggle, 164
Daimoku, 173; advancement through, 83; source of development, 62; source of fortune, 170; strength of, 71; tone of, 65
deadlock, 39, 156, 173, 199; in organization, 51
decision-making, 113
democracy, 12, 54, 118, 219
desires, 125
destiny, change, 82, 192, 207 234; also see karma
destructive attitudes, 182
determination, 63, 74, 131, 168, 215, 258; in business, 223; in crucial moment, 84; renewal of, 97; to make someone happy, 54
development, 36; as capable men, 76, 211; in youth, 192; of leaders, 29, 86; of members, 81; of outlying areas, 40; organizational, 56; source of, 63, 173; also see self-development
dignity, 34, 35, 223; of youth 92
diplomacy, 190
direction, 52; of campaigns, 172; of faith, 152, 207

281

disciples, standards for, 217; also see master-disciple
discussion meetings, 204; atmosphere of, 61, 66, 109; emcee, 181
dismissals, of leaders, 50, 161
dissatisfaction, with job, 221
doubt, 173, 180
dreams, 203; realization of, 267; sharing, 175; also see hopes

economics, 257; also see budgeting, finances, and money
education, 191; going to college, 239; importance of, 102; Soka University, 256
effort, 138, 261; at work, 211; in Shakubuku, 136; to overcome circumstances, 200; unseen, 119, 211
elderly members, giving guidance to, 57; understanding, 81
eloquence, 192, 204
emcee, 181
encouragement, 30, 52, 89, 155, 204, 209; through experience, 61; to dismissed leaders, 50; also see guidance
endurance, 146
enjoyment, of practice, 153, 232; also see practice
enlightenment, attainment of, 149, 183, 206
environment, determined by attitude, 99

envy, 249
Esho Funi, 75, 116, 134, 170 266
examples, 46, 67, 72, 94; setting, 45
expediency, 83

failure, 175
fairness, 53
faith, 50, 182, 199, 201, 245; advancement of, 83, 89, 146, 156; and position 50, 62, 248; and study, 170; direction of, 152, 207; equals daily life, 147, 224; first, 103, 143, 193, 205; fundamental mission, 12; in daily life, 106, 168, 174; is a seeking mind, 218; is confidence, 155; is courage, 103; is Daimoku, 136; is *Ichinen*, 106; is practice, 143; is unity, 220; keys to, 168; leads to *enlightenment*, 183; not criticizing, 180; obstacles to, 95; only real treasure, 182; related to marriage, 233; relation to Gongyo, 174; strength of, 77, 140; throughout lifetime, 184; understanding of, 163; vs. fame, wealth, etc., 182; vs. self-assertiveness, 215; without practice, 165; also see practice
false pride, 174; also see pretense
fame, transience of, 163, 182,

family, 141, 214, 240, 235; consideration, 194

fearlessness, 114; also see courage

feminine beauty, 229, 230

finances, 51, 229

flattery, 109

following, 90; guidance, 88, 164

formality, 17, 33, 47, 173; at meetings, 109; of guidance 38

fortitude, 208

fortune, 23, 110, 152; basis of happiness, 170; depends on faith, 149; gaining, 232; lack of, 116

friendship, 121; bonds of, 73; good friends in Buddhism, 144

fusion, with Gohonzon, 144

future, hopes in, 79; unreliability of, 238

Gakkai spirit, 59, 78, 84, 94, 138; never changing, 134

generosity, 35, 53

goals, 194, 231; in marriage, 233; setting of, 99

Gongyo, 174, 230; and voice, 179

grooming, personal, 229

guidance, ability to give, 36; atmosphere of, 109; concreteness of, 61; essence 21; flexibility of, 106, following, 88, 164; for youth, 32, 194, 234; giving, 17, 21, 28, 34, 46, 54, 82, 88, 93, 207; on Shakubuku, 125; & voice, 263; receiving, 61, 94, 174, 194; responsibility in, 215; spirit of giving, 39; strictness of, 40; to elderly members, 57; to outlying areas, 40

happiness, ability to attain, 98, 170; for others, 54, 172; in marriage, 233; instinctive desire, 187; in faith, 168, 236

hardships, 161, 200, 220; fear of, 162; also see obstacles

harmony, 64, 119

health, 96, 188, 236

Hendoku Iyaku, 50, 175

heroes, 64, 105, 118

high spirits, 179

history, 273

Hon'in-myo, 79, 97, 156, 168

Honmatsu Kukyo-to, 34, 71, 173

Honmon-Shakumon, 161, 172 age of, 110

hope, 199; accomplishment of, 195; also see dreams

Hosshaku Kempon, 156

humanism, 11, 32, 117, 209, 259; and leadership, 16; of leaders, 77

human revolution, 134, 200; attainment of, 37, 74, 99; depends on faith, 149; perfect nature, 188; proof of, 91

Ichinen, 71, 162; awareness through, 165; determines happiness, 153; during campaigns, 202; during illness, 96; effect of, 93; of leaders, 121; to the Gohonzon, 106, 185; towards members, 97
Ichinen Sanzen, 212, 218, 269; core of life, 75
ideology, unification of, 137
illness, 96, 189, 236
impartiality, 16, 107
individuality, 65, 209, 268; a matter of destiny, 103
Inga Guji, see cause and effect
initiative, 86, 136; creation 47; to develop leaders, 27
insight, 22, 55
inspiration, 48, 61; to practice, 162
introspection, 51, 206
Itai Doshin, see unity

jealousy, 63
Jigyo Keta, 229; see practice, for self and others
Jikkai, see *ten worlds*
journalism, 270
judgment, 13, 16, 19, 25, 41, 76, 109, 119, 212; of Buddhism, 181; of character, 53; of person's value, 102, 117, 161; poor, 193

karma, 103, 138; change, 200, 243; also see destiny

Kyochi Myogo, 144, 154
Kosen-rufu, attainment of, 119, 136, 195; basis of, 199; conviction towards, 39, 92; golden age, 148; humanistic society, 259; mission of youth, 213; music and, 260; requires courage, 15

lagging, 156
leaders, 12, 21, 33, 53, 55, 106; attitude of, 48, 74, 94, 107; character of, 12, 77, 92; conduct of, 95; development of, 29, 86; evaluating people, 20; *Ichinen*, 77, 121; practice of, 46, 71, 94, 142; raising, 26, 79; reason for, 17; responsibilities, 76, 119, 131, 230; standards for, 17; unity of, 18; understanding people, 19; and common people, 77,118,265; wives of, 48; women, 230, 243
learning, 124
life, is *Ichinen Sanzen*, 218
lifetime practice, 78, 79, 184; also see consistence
literature, 274
love, for parents, 194;

M.C., see emcee
marriage, 233; wives as leaders, 241; husband-wife relationship, 48, 205, 235
master-disciple, 73, 84, 123,

144, 152, 161, 177, 217
meetings, see discussion meetings
members, loans among, 147; raising, 55; reflections of leaders, 54; should be treasured, 108; training of, 175
memories, 230; of struggles 201
memory, 257
mercy, 17, 41, 43, 57; guidance is, 82; vs. love, 244
mission, 171; realization of, 12, 29, 31, 102, 247
money, 182, 232; loans to members, 147
motherhood, 240, 241
music, 266, 274; of the Third Civilization, 260

nature, 188
negligence, 121
Ninpo Ikka, see person and Law
non-members, relationship to, 255

objectivity, 20
obstacles, 96, 125, 133, 175, 194, 200, 216; defeating, 189; fight or retreat, 271; necessity of, 164; to faith, 95
opinions, 20; public, 19
opportunity, 140
onshitsu, 143, 154
organization, purity of, 147; reason for, 97, 101; role 138

overreaching, 174, 231

parents, concern for, 194
passion, 39, 46, 265; for day's work, 196; of youth, 105

passivity, 162
past, present and future, 79
patience, 17, 138
patriotism, 102
perceptiveness, 20, 24, 28, 41, 121
perseverance, 74, 97, 155, 202; in practice, 73, 205; with Gakkai spirit, 59; toward Kosen-rufu, 92; with members, 43; also see persistence
persistence, 120, 136, 199; in work, 224;
person and Law, oneness of, 176
personality, 27
philosophy, Buddhist-Western 255; confusion of, 137; behind effort, 120; means of fulfilling desires, 254; of happiness, 118; tolerance of others, 52, 137, 253
physical appearance, 96
pioneer spirit, 148, 216
planning, 48, 58, 59, 133
politics, 257, 264
position, and faith, 50, 62; promotion, 248; removal from, 161
positive spirit, 92, 162
practicality, 60, 203

285

practice, 143; better than theory, 165; consistency of, 79, 172, 205; ensures benefits, 146; for own sake, 138; for self and others, 88, 229; inspiration to, 162; is voluntary, 172, leaders', 71; lifetime, 79, 181, 184; necessary for *enlightenment*, 125; perfects nature, 188; self-centered, 162; simplicity of, 150; strength of, 266; with joy, 220; see faith
praise, 16, 81, 94
prejudice, 195
press, 270
pretense, 91, 214, 265; be yourself, 65, 73, 82, 223; as leaders, 17, 33, 268
pride, see pretense
problems, see obstacles
promptness, 56, 76
prosperity, 254
protection, 56; by the Gohonzon, 218; of *Shoten Zenjin*, 138; of members, 74
purpose, see mission
public opinion, 19, 269

questions, see seeking mind

racial discrimination, 195
rapture, 168, 169
reading, 271, 272
relationship, of husband and wife, 48, 205; with Buddhism, 141; with juniors, 44; with non-members, 225; with society, 223; also see master-disciple
reports, 41, 129
respect, 44, 90, 209
responsibility, 13, 41, 86, 88; in giving guidance, 215; of leaders, 76, 119, 131, 230; social, 186, 239
results, 45
revolution, of values, 199; peaceful, 133; through Shakubuku, 136; also see human revolution
rhythm, 202; steady, 172
rumors, 109

sacrifice, 133
Sansho Shima, see obstacles
schedules, need for, 55
scholars, 259
science, and Buddhism, 254
scolding, 57, 81; act of, 115
seeking mind, 61, 82, 162, 187, 216
self-awakening, 28, 176, 178
self-confidence, see confidence
self-development, 62, 75, 86, 117, 192, 268; consistent, 173
self-satisfaction, 31, 131
Shakubuku, 125, 204; cheerful, 92; difficulty of, 138; effort of, 136; greatest joy 239; in outlying areas, 45; source of benefit, 142; spirit of, 134; supporting, 45; through conduct, 95

Shitei Funi, see master-disciple

Shoten Zenjin, see Buddhist gods

shyness, 192

sincerity, 35, 53, 57, 98, 151, 161, 204, 207, 265, 269

slander, of Gohonzon, 180; of true Buddhism, 110

sleep, 202

Soka University, 256

solitary, Bodhisattva, 131; practice, 89

spirit, 179; Gakkai, 78, 84, 94, 134, 138; of activities, 77; of women, 248; of youth, 196; pioneer, 148; positive, 162; youthful, 105, 214, 216, 275

stand alone, 33, 78, 131, 142, 210; sign of true hero, 105

strategy, in activities, 133; in business, 223

strength, development of, 162 during hardships, 168, of character, 201, 208; of Daimoku, 71; of faith, 77, 115; of practice, 266

study, 261, 271; and activities, 170; importance of, 26, of Buddhism, 191

success, 164, 211, 268

support, at work, 224; in Shakubuku, 45

ten worlds, 274

timing, 56, 84, 101, 110, 140

theory, vs. practice, 165, 172

training, 27, 29; of members, 175; of young men's division, 126; strict, 126; also see guidance

traveling, 195

true aspect, 156

trust, 248; being trusted, 38, 192, 221, 265; during youth, 192; in Gohonzon, 218; master-disciple, 161

understanding, 55, 88; of elderly members, 81; of faith, 163

unity, 89, 106, 155, 195; among members, 73; benefit from, 150; communication, 131; creation of, 47; is faith, 268; key to victory, 128; organizational, 127, 132, 140; to attain Kosen-rufu, 155

value, creation of, 48, 207 (s) 22; pursuit of transient, 163

victory, 131; achievement of, 85

vitality, 202, 249; of organization, 177; through faith, 15; through goals, 100; in Shakubuku, 138

voice, 263; in Gongyo, 179

weakness, 89, 115, 162; hidden, 105; not hindrance, 30

widows, 244, 245

win or lose, 114, 151, 201

winning, 131, 136, 151, 164,

wisdom, 38, 55, 68, 193, 201, 271; and good fortune, 22; application of, 207; quality of greatness, 126; from faith, 14

wives, listening to, 48; seven kinds, 237; also see women

women, 233; beauty of, 229; chapter chiefs, 248; courage of, 250; leaders, 231, 243, 247; liberation, 247; mission, 247; mothers, 240, 241; spirit of, 248; youthful, 241, 246

work, 185, 221, 224; and activities, 166, 172

worrying, 235, 238; see obstacles

writing, 261, 262, 269

youth, 32, 194, 201, 202; and music, 266; character of, 73; dignity of, 92; Daimoku of, 196; development of, 212; future of, 212; mission of, 213; passion of, 105; spirit of, 214, 216, 223, 275; take responsibility, 196; time for foundation, 162, 167, 234 also see spirit; and leaders

Zenchishiki, 59
Zuiho Bini, 134